Remaining Catholic

Remaining Catholic

Six Good Reasons for Staying in an Imperfect Church

Martin Pable, OFM Cap.

ASSISTING CHRISTIANS TO ACT

PUBLICATIONS

Remaining Catholic
Six Good Reasons for Staying in an Imperfect Church
by Martin Pable, OFM Cap.

Edited by Andrew Yankech
Cover Design by Tom A. Wright
Typesetting by Desktop Edit Shop, Inc.

Scripture quotations are from the *New Revised Standard Version of the Bible*, copyright © 1989 by the Division of Christian Education of the National Council of the Church of Christ in the USA. All rights reserved. Used by permission.

Published by   ACTA Publications
                 Assisting Christians to Act
                 5559 W. Howard St.
                 Skokie, IL 60077
                 800-397-2282
                 www.actapublications.com

Library of Congress Catalog Number: 2005926201
ISBN: 0-87946-289-2
Printed in the United States of America
Year: 12 11 10 09 08 07 06
Printing: 10 9 8 7 6 5 4 3 2

Contents

I would like to dedicate this book to some very special people in my life:

- *to my parents, whose example of prayer and Christian living grounded me in my journey of faith;*

- *to my parochial school teachers, the Sisters of St. Agnes, who instilled in me a love for the Catholic religion;*

- *to my Capuchin brothers and seminary professors, who helped me make the transition to post-Vatican II theology;*

- *and finally, to the many people who have shared with me their doubts and struggles to find a meaningful faith in the complex world of our time.*

Preface

For better or for worse, the problems of the Catholic Church draw a great deal of scrutiny from the media. The scandals arising from clergy sexual misconduct are the most obvious example, but there are also the internal conflicts and divisions within the church, the downturn in Mass attendance, and the abuses of power that sometimes alienate church members.

In the face of these problems, some Catholics have decided they want nothing more to do with the church. They have affiliated themselves with some other denomination or religion or have simply dropped out of organized religion altogether. This book will probably not speak to them. But there are other Catholics who are pained by what they see happening in the church. Some have stopped participating, yet they still think of themselves as Catholics and may consider reconnecting if they believe some things have changed and they would be welcomed back. Some are not practicing themselves but want some religious formation for their children. Others are in a second or third marriage and are not sure what it would take for them to return. Still others have honest disagreements with the church about contraception, abortion, homosexuality, the authority of the pope, and so on, or have been offended or traumatized by the treatment they received at the hands of a priest, a sister, or some other church member, yet they still have an open mind.

My hope is that reading this book may open an inviting door for all of the above to take another look at the church. Perhaps they will discover that the church today has a different face from the one they experienced earlier in life. For those who have been hurt, I would like to offer a sincere apology for whatever pain they may have experienced. I have always believed that people have a great sense of fairness and that giving someone or something "another look" or "another chance" appeals to that sense.

There are two other groups for whom this book is intended. For one, there are people who are not Catholic but have a good bit of curiosity about the church. They have heard conflicting messages from different people about what the church teaches, and they are not ready to check out a Catholic encyclopedia or website to find clarity. I would hope that this small book may provide some insight and prompt them to continue their search. And finally, there is a fairly large group of practicing Catholics who are themselves somewhat confused about the church or have friends who question them about their beliefs.

This book is not a substitute for *The Catechism of the Catholic Church* or other authoritative sources. It is a modest attempt to explain why, despite its many problems and failures, people continue to find strong reasons for staying, joining or returning to the Catholic Church. I will be happy to dialogue further with anyone who wishes to follow up on the matters covered in this book through the website of the St. Anthony Retreat Center: www.sarcenter.com.

Fr. Martin Pable, OFM Cap.

Reason #1

Community

Why Do We Need a Church Anyway?

One of the more frequently asked questions regarding religion nowadays is "Why do we need a church anyway?" It is not a frivolous question. We live in a postmodern society that questions the necessity and relevance of any institution. Moreover, the attitudes and behaviors of the churches have given added impetus to the cynicism about them. The sexual abuse scandals among the clergy, the heavy-handed use of authority, the pretentiousness of some church buildings, news stories of fiscal mismanagement—all have contributed to the feeling that churches may be a hindrance rather than a doorway to union with God.

It is because of feelings like this that we often hear people say things like: "I'm spiritual but not religious." "I have a relationship with God (or Jesus), but I don't go to church." "I pray to God by myself. I don't need those boring, repetitious prayers and songs you hear in church." "I just read the Bible and try to live a good life—I can do that without the church, thank you." "I find God when I'm walking in the woods or sitting at the lakeshore—that's my church."

Devout, church-going people are often at a loss as to how

to respond to these statements—especially when they come from good, sincere, and morally upright people. So let me try to suggest some answers or at least some directions for thinking them through. I will begin with a couple of substantive, theological reflections and then follow with a few pragmatic replies based on human experience.

First, we need to be clear on a key point: What is the goal of religion or spirituality? I think we can agree that it is not simply good feelings or even right living. These may be important, but they are not the ultimate goal. "Begin with the end in mind" is one of Stephen Covey's *Seven Habits of Highly Effective People* (Free Press, 2004). The "end" of all religion is *union with God and with the human family.* If that is the case, then we need to follow God's way or plan for spiritual living, not our own. It is clear from the Bible that God's plan is for people to find blessedness, happiness and union with God not merely as individuals but as part of a community. One of the key concepts in Scripture is that of *covenant*: "I will be your God, and you will be my people." The covenant was with the entire community of Israel. God promised to love them and care for them and to be willing to forgive them and take them back even when they proved fickle and unfaithful. It was this unfailing, consistent, unconditional love of God that kept the Israelite community together even when they were besieged by enemies and dragged off into captivity.

> *God's plan is for people to find blessedness, happiness and union with God not merely as individuals but as part of a community.*

Moreover, God gave Moses directives on how the people were to pray and worship God. They were to pray as individuals. But even more, they were expected to join in the worship of the entire community. In that sense, they were truly a church. As far as I know, no one in Old Testament times ever challenged this arrangement. The Israelites would not think of separating themselves from the covenant community. That would be tantamount to spiritual death. Indeed, to be excluded (excommunicated) from the community was the severest form of punishment, short of physical death.

Jesus and Community

The New Testament portrays Jesus as a devout, practicing member of the Jewish community. An early indication of this is found in the Gospel of Luke. Jesus has just returned from his temptations in the desert and is beginning his public ministry. He came to his home town of Nazareth and "went to the synagogue on the Sabbath day, *as was his custom*" (Luke 4:16; emphasis mine). From this we can deduce that Jesus was not a spiritual loner or a maverick striking out on an individualistic spiritual quest. No, he was a faithful, practicing member of his Jewish community, deeply inserted into the religious traditions and prayer forms of his people. The words "as was his custom" indicate that Jesus had formed the habit of regular synagogue worship, very likely through the example and training of his devout parents. True, the Gospels often show him praying individually, but they are equally clear about his connection with regular synagogue worship and observance of the traditional Jewish religious feasts. (As I sometimes tell people, if going to church was important for Jesus, it's good enough for me!)

As Jesus began to collect his disciples, he worked hard to form them into a community. Being human, they each had their petty agendas and ambitions that threatened their cohesiveness. So he continually had to challenge their jockeying for favoritism and privilege (Mark 9:33-37; Matthew 20:20-28). He asked them to renounce all forms of domination and to think of themselves as servants of others (Luke 22:24-27; John 13:1217). The night before he died, Jesus begged his Father to bring all believers into unity and to end the divisions in the human family (John 17:20-23). Then he instituted the great sacrament of unity, the Holy Eucharist, to be both the sign and the cause of unity among the members of the church. He called it "the new covenant." But it is the same wonderful promise: "I am your God, and you are my beloved people."

After his death and resurrection, Jesus continued to instruct his disciples and help them understand their mission: to continue what he had begun. Just before his ascension, he "commissioned" them to go out and bring his message into the whole world (Matthew 28:16-20). On Pentecost Sunday, after Peter told the story of Jesus' life, death and resurrection, the people said, "If all this is true, what should we do?" Peter did not say, "Well, just accept Jesus as your personal savior and have a nice day." He said, "Repent and be baptized, every one of you, in the name of Jesus Christ, so that your sins may be forgiven; and you will receive the gift of the Holy Spirit" (Acts 2:38). Note the elements here:

- "Repent"—acknowledge that you are a sinner, that you need conversion and change of heart.

There are some disorders in your life that need reordering. This is a far cry from the "cheap grace" we often hear of today: "I'm OK—you're OK." Becoming a disciple of Jesus means we have some interior work to do.

- "And be baptized"—this powerful ritual signifies that the new follower of Christ is willing to let go of past ways of thinking and acting and to begin a new life patterned on the life of Jesus. Moreover, it includes the intention to become a member of this Christian community, where everyone is expected to care for one another, not just for themselves (Acts 2:44-45; 4:34-35).

- "You will receive the gift of the Holy Spirit"—you will be empowered to use your gifts and talents to help build up the human family into a community of love and care. And you will be given courage to act with confidence even in the face of opposition.

This was the lived experience of those first Christians. There was no individualist spirituality here, no sense of "I don't need any connection with a church in order to connect with God." The emphasis was clearly on being bonded with the community, praying together, and caring for one another: "They devoted themselves to the apostles' teaching and fellowship, to the breaking of bread and the prayers" (Acts 2:42).

As we read the Acts of the Apostles and the letters of Peter, Paul and John, we see this basic pattern of communal spirituality unfolding and becoming ever clearer. Whenever the apostles succeeded in bringing people to faith in Christ, they would form them into communities. These began to be called "churches," from the Greek word *ekklesia*, meaning "called out" or "called apart." The communities saw themselves as separated both from the pagan temples and from the Jewish synagogues. They had a structure. They were presided over by persons variously called elders, presbyters or bishops. Other members exercised diverse ministries such as teacher, evangelist, prophet, healer and caregiver to the poor (Romans 12:4-8; 1 Corinthians 12:4-11). A favorite image used by Saint Paul was that of the church as "the body of Christ." Each and every member of the body was important, even though they had different functions or roles. Together they formed an organic unity with Christ as the head. In such a view, there was no room for jealousy, for arrogance, for competitiveness, or for sniping at one another. All these create divisions in the body (1 Corinthians 1:10-13; Philippians 2:1-4).

The church is so significant that Jesus died on the cross for it.

I recently read *The Purpose-Driven Life* (Zondervan, 2002), the fine book by Protestant pastor Rick Warren. In it he devotes the whole of chapter seventeen to the importance of Christians belonging to a church community. The chapter begins, "You are called to belong, not just believe." This is in sharp contrast with the contemporary phenomenon of "believing without belonging" noted by researcher George Gallup. Warren draws heavily upon the Scriptures to demonstrate that God's plan for our salvation includes belonging to a church. "Membership in the family of God is neither inconsequential nor something to be casually ignored," he writes. "The church is God's agenda for the world. Jesus said, 'I will build my church, and all the powers of hell will not conquer it' (Matthew 16:18). The church is so significant that Jesus died on the cross for it: 'Christ loved the church and gave his life for it' (Ephesians 5:25). The Bible calls the church 'the bride of Christ' and 'the body of Christ.' I can't imagine saying to Jesus, 'I love you, but I dislike your wife.' Or 'I accept you, but I reject your body.'"

Warren then goes on to offer some biblically-based "compelling reasons" for being committed and active in a local church community: A church family moves us out of self-centered isolation. The body of Christ needs us and our gifts. We will share in Christ's mission in the world. A church family will keep us from backsliding. He concludes: "Why is it important to join a local church family? Because it proves you are committed to your spiritual brothers and sisters in reality, not just in theory. God wants you to love *real* people, not *ideal* people. You can spend a lifetime searching for the perfect church, but you will never find it. You are called to love imperfect sinners, just as God does."

Church and Human Experience

So why do we need a church? Primarily because that is God's design for spiritual living. And we, being human creatures, are called to follow God's design, not create our own. Of course, if one does not accept the authority of the Bible or of Christian history, that logic will not be persuasive. So let's look at the question from another perspective: human experience. That may enable us to reply to some of the objections to church affiliation that we raised at the beginning of this book.

For example, "I'm spiritual but not religious" has become a slogan for many today. I think I understand what they are trying to say: "I believe there is a God, and I pray and try to live a good life. But I don't believe you have to go to church, practice religious rituals, or obey a bunch of rules in order to be a spiritual person." That is surely not an unreasonable attitude, especially when the speaker is leading a morally upright life. At the same time, I believe the distinction between "spiritual" and "religious" creates a needless dichotomy. The Latin root of the word religion literally means "to bind together." Religion at its best has the power to forge bonds between the individual and God and between the individual and other persons. It can bind the human community together in worship of the Supreme Being, and it can link them together in mutual love, respect and care. That is a powerful force for good.

My concern for people who hold this view is that they are missing out on much that can help them to live spiritually. They have no sense of tradition, no historical memory of a community that has lived through generations of struggle and victory, of sin and repentance, of cowardice and heroism, and of joy and sorrow. George Gallup describes them as "spiritual loners." They have no shared vision of meaning and purpose for living or for dealing with the tragedies and absurdities of life. And apart from their circle of friends, they have no community of faith and prayer to support them through their times of loss and pain.

Another objection to church affiliation is "I just read the Bible and try to live a good life. I can do that without the church." True enough, at least in theory. But people like this will be missing the same spiritual supports as were noted above. Have you ever tried to embark on a regular physical exercise program by yourself? Or a weight loss program? Or a daily practice of yoga or meditation? After a good start, most of us find ourselves slipping away—unless we have a companion or two who will pull us along and remotivate us when our own resolve starts to lag.

It is much the same in the spiritual life. When we want to deepen our relationship with God, come to know the Bible better, or commit ourselves to a work of mercy, it is far easier to stick with it if we have the support of other like-minded people. That is the gift of a church community. Each week we gather to hear the Word of God proclaimed and its message applied to our own concerns and struggles. We offer prayers and sing hymns that remind us of timeless truths that can so easily be forgotten in the bustle of daily life. We receive spiritual strength and nourishment from the living body and blood of Christ in the Holy Eucharist, because we know we cannot rely on our own resources alone. We find out how our fellow Christians are doing, and we know we can ask their prayers if we are going through a tough time. And during the week, in most parish communities, there are opportunities for study, for shared prayer and fellowship, and for service to others.

All these are, I believe, weighty reasons for wanting to be part of a church community, which is why Jesus, in his great wisdom, founded a church to continue his work of redeeming and sanctifying our world. It strikes me that movements such as Alcoholics Anonymous and their derivatives have recognized the healing and sustaining power of group membership. Interestingly, psychologist Martin Seligman links the rise of depression in our time to the rise of individualism and the erosion of community support systems in the culture. In our contemporary world where so many people are suffering from loneliness and isolation, a caring, vibrant church community can truly be a light in the darkness.

Problems with Church

I have tried to address an important question that thoughtful people today are raising: "Why do we need a church in order to live spiritually? Why can't I do it on my own?" I began by pointing out the priority of viewing the question from God's side rather than from our own. That is: What is God's plan or design for our spiritual well-being? And I replied with the biblical testimony: God desires to be sought-found-worshipped-served in the context of community. I made the further point that this arrangement corresponds remarkably well with our human nature. We are "hardwired" for connection with one another. We are born into a human community (the family) and nurtured there. We seek friendships and even intimate relationships with one another. One of our deepest sufferings arises from the feeling of being alone and abandoned. It would be strange indeed if our spiritual life—that which is most human about us—would follow some other dynamic: individualism. No, our quest for God is intimately bound up with our human relationships, which is why Jesus founded a church. It is there that we are to pursue our own spiritual development and at the same time contribute to the strengthening of the human family according to God's purposes.

It is, however, no secret that a large number of people have walked away from the church or have no desire to connect with it. Part of the problem is that the church often falls far short of what Christ intended it to be. History is strewn with the church's failures. Popes and bishops have too often acted more like secular princes than as servants of Jesus Christ. A host of evils can be paraded before our eyes: the persecution of Jews, the forced conversion of native peoples during colonial times, the abuses and excesses of the Inquisition, and the violent reaction to Martin Luther and the other Protestant reformers. In our own time, we have seen the terrible scandals and cover-ups discovered by the recent revelations of clergy sexual abuse, the censorship of theologians and biblical scholars, and the refusal of bishops and pastors to dialogue with laypeople about pastoral concerns.

It is no secret that a large number of people have walked away from the church, or have no desire to connect with it.

It is not an unfair question to ask: "Why should anyone want to join the Catholic Church—or remain in it?" It is not my intention in this book to "recruit" people for the church. As I stated in the Preface, I simply want to lift up some of the aspects of Catholic life that people may not understand very well or may have forgotten. First, let me remind readers that they already belong to or are part of many institutions that are flawed. As a psychologist, for example, I am acutely aware of the violations of ethical standards by some practitioners. Also, there are major divisions within the profession over various theories of human behavior, the effectiveness of psychotherapy, the use of mind-altering drugs, and so on. Still I do not hesitate to identify myself as a psychologist, because I believe that the science of psychology has great potential to improve human life. Similarly, people who belong to unions or corporations are well aware of the inequities, the infighting, the clash of egos, and other unsavory aspects of the organization. But they stay with it because, overall, they find more good than evil there. In fact, as Americans we are sometimes ashamed by or in disagreement with some of our nation's policies and decisions. But we do not therefore renounce our citizenship.

> *I do not hesitate to identify myself as a psychologist, because I believe that the science of psychology has great potential to improve human life.*

Why should it be any different with the church? Perhaps some people will say, "Yes, but the church ought to be different. It should be a bright light shining in the darkness. It should not simply mirror the flaws of the secular institutions."

It is hard to argue with that. I have often felt deep pain in my own heart when I see the church acting more like a business corporation than "a communion of persons united in the love of Christ"—which is Pope John Paul II's favorite image for the church. But the sober truth is that Jesus did not found a perfect church. He founded a church with both divine and human faces. The divine element is his own abiding presence in the church: "I am with you always, to the end of the age" (Matthew 28:20), and the wisdom and guidance of the Holy Spirit that Jesus has poured out upon the church: "The Holy Spirit, whom the Father will send in my name, will

22

teach you everything, and remind you of all that I have said to you" (John 14:26).

The Human Face of the Church

The human face of the church is not always pretty. The members of the church, including its leaders, are flawed human beings. Some are remarkably mature and holy. Others are petty, self-serving, and ego-driven. All are "subject to weakness," as the Letter to the Hebrews says (5:2). That is why the church is never fully what it should be. The Second Vatican Council, in one of its memorable moments, proclaimed the church to be "holy yet always in need of reform." The church is neither totally perfect nor wholly corrupt. To use a popular expression, it is "a mixed bag." Some Catholics have great difficulty accepting this truth. If they could accept the tension between these two poles, they would be more at peace with the church.

The other day I was reading the end of the Gospel of Mark where Jesus commissions the disciples: "Go into all the world and proclaim the good news to the whole creation" (16:15). But I was struck by the verse just preceding it: "He upbraided [scolded] them for their lack of faith and stubbornness," because they had refused to believe the reports about his resurrection. Jesus could have said, "Since you guys are so stuck in your own disillusion and cynicism, I'm going to select and train a whole new core of disciples. Be off with you!" Instead, in an amazing act of confidence in these flawed and fickle people, he goes ahead and commissions them to continue his mission until the end of time. I find that comforting. From the very beginning, Jesus knew his church would be entrusted into fragile hands.

Didn't things change after Pentecost, however, when the Holy Spirit's gifts were poured out on the community? Yes—but not in the sense of creating a perfect church. The human element remained. That is why we find statements like "the Hellenists [Greek-speaking Christians] complained against the Hebrews because their widows were being neglected in the daily distribution of food" (Acts 6:1). In other words, there was favoritism going on, and people were complaining. But instead of letting the situation deteriorate, the apostles used the occasion to create a new ministry in the community. They chose and ordained seven deacons to take charge of distributing food to the needy. Later on we read that some church leaders began demanding that the new Gentile converts be circumcised. But "Paul and Barnabas had no small dissension and debate with them" (Acts 15:1-2). Once again, instead of allowing the dispute to fester and cause division, the community agreed to meet together to discuss the issue in the spirit of prayer and invocation of the Holy Spirit. Together they found a pastoral solution that everyone could agree on. Even Peter and Paul had arguments with each other (Galatians 2:11-14), but they worked it out. Neither one ever walked away from the community.

As time went on, the Christian church had to deal with disputes and disagreements in every period of history. For the first three centuries of its existence, there was not even agreement on which writings belonged in the Bible. That finally got settled at the Council of Rome in 392. Indeed, nearly all the statements in the creed we profess at Mass each Sunday are the fruit of ecumenical councils that were called to settle theological disputes—with good people on both sides of every question. This is a remarkable testimony to the power of the Holy Spirit to guide the church "to all truth" as Jesus had promised.

❖ ❖ ❖

Why Do We Stay?

With this history of disagreement, we should not be surprised to find factions, disputes and scandals in today's Catholic Church. My Protestant friends have assured me that the situation is similar in their churches. They remain committed, however, because they find so much that is good in their communities. Sometimes I ask my Catholic lay friends, "What keeps *you* in this messy church?" Their answers have been very instructive.

They remain committed, however, because they find so much that is good in their communities.

Some speak of the high quality of the Sunday liturgy at their parish. People are greeted warmly at the door. The priest goes out of his way to extend a welcome to everyone, including visitors. He truly prays the great texts of the Mass in a way that draws the people into prayer. The congregation joins in the singing and appears to enjoy doing so because the music expresses their faith and touches their hearts. The lectors don't just read the Scriptures—they proclaim them with reverence and conviction. The homily draws people in and helps them see how the Scriptures speak to their own life experience. After Mass, people don't rush out and practically run each other down in the parking lot. They stay to mingle with each other and talk about how their lives are going. Not every Sunday liturgy is such a spiritual rush, but, generally, people leave with a sense that Christ is truly present to them in the everyday aspects of their lives.

Generally people leave [Mass] with a sense that Christ is truly present to them in the everyday aspects of their lives.

Others appreciate the fact that the pope is such a visible symbol of the church's unity and universality. They value his willingness to be physically present to people of different races and cultures across the world. They applaud his strong stand on the dignity and human rights of every person and his courage to publicly disagree with powerful world leaders on difficult issues, such as abortion, capital punishment, and unjust warfare. They may not agree with everything he says, but they respect him as a prophetic voice in a world obsessed with consumption and exploitation of the powerless.

Still others are attracted by the educational and charitable missions of the church. Whatever theological or pastoral differences they may have, many admire the church for its 2000 years of history of trying to better the human condition through education, health care, strengthening of family life, and efforts to win just treatment for victims of unfair social and economic arrangements. Going beyond admiration, an increasing number of Catholics are willing to become personally involved in continuing the church's mission. I am always in awe when I visit parishes and see how many people are giving their time and energy as council and committee members, liturgical ministers, catechists, visitors to the sick and homebound, jail and prison ministers, youth ministers, and volunteers in food programs, shelters and missions to poor people in this country and abroad. They have a strong sense that they are not doing anything heroic but simply living out the call of their baptism: to make the love of Christ present and visible in the world.

I receive many other replies to my question, "What keeps you in the Catholic Church?" Some are inspired by the church's patronage of the arts. They are awed by the great Byzantine basilicas with their wonderful mosaics and icons depicting the mysteries of faith and the saints who embodied them, or the majestic cathedrals of Europe with their magnificent stained-glass windows that served for centuries as visual catechisms for people who could not read, or the enormous repertoire of music inspired by the Bible or the liturgy. Even as I am writing this, the radio in my room is playing Hector Berlioz's beautiful *Requiem*. And how many of the world's great paintings are based on scenes from the life of Jesus, Mary, Old Testament figures, and lives of the saints?

Finally, people tell me things like: "The church provides moral guidance for my children." "I have access to a whole world of spiritual writings that have come down to us through the centuries." "When my life was out of control, it was a Catholic coworker who reminded me that I could find God's forgiveness and strength for a new start by making a good confession." "There have been times in my life when the only thing that kept me going was knowing that Jesus was there for me in Holy Communion."

These people are not naive. They know very well that the

Catholic Church is a body with many warts, wounds and scars. They know there is often a disconnect between what it teaches and how it acts. They are not afraid to be critical of the church when they perceive inconsistencies and injustices. But through it all, they continue to look beyond the human face to see the deeper reality: It is still the church of Jesus Christ, his body extended in space and time "for us and for our salvation."

Tradition and History

The Church Has a Long Memory

One of the highlights of the past year for me was my pilgrimage to Greece and Turkey "in the footsteps of Saint Paul." It was a trip to the ancient places of Athens, Corinth, Thessalonica, Philippi, Pergamum, Ephesus—all places where Paul preached and founded church communities. Standing amid those ruins of what were once thriving commercial cities gave me a profound sense of being connected with the ancient Christian world. These places, as well as so many others in the Mediterranean region, were the sites where the apostles and the first missionaries brought the gospel of Christ to the people. One of the high points of our pilgrimage was celebrating Mass outdoors at the stream near Philippi where Paul baptized Lydia, the first convert to Christianity on European soil. Together we renewed our own baptismal vows, and we felt a deep sense of historical continuity with the early church.

In recent years a number of Protestant pastors and teachers have found their way into the Catholic Church, mostly by going back and studying the early history of the church. Scott Hahn, for example, began his ministerial career as a Presbyterian seminary teacher who used every opportunity to portray the corrupt nature of the Catholic Church and its teachings. But he was always troubled by the tendency of Protestantism to splinter into factions and separate church bodies. At the time of his writing about his own spiritual journey (*Rome Sweet Home*, Ignatius Press, 1993), he noted that there were more than 25,000 different Protestant denominations, each one claiming to be following the Holy Spirit and "the plain meaning of [S]cripture." Can any of these legitimately claim to be "the true church of Jesus Christ?" Can any of them demonstrate historical continuity with the church of the apostles?

> *He noted that there were more than 25,000 different Protestant denominations, each one claiming to be following the Holy Spirit and "the plain meaning of [S]cripture."*

Questions like these, plus the challenges of some of his students, led Hahn to an intensive study of the New Testament and early church history. To his initial dismay, this endeavor served only to validate the claims of the Catholic Church that he had previously attacked: the necessity of church tradition for knowledge of the true faith, not "the Bible alone" as Luther and the first Reformers had taught; the crucial importance of the papacy and the college of bishops to insure unity and doctrinal orthodoxy; and the real presence of Christ in the sacrament of the Eucharist. Eventually, he became a Catholic and is now one of the most scholarly and eloquent proponents of Catholic teaching in this country.

Another example of someone who discovered (or rather rediscovered) the church through the study of history is Jeff

Cavins. He shares his spiritual journey in his book *My Life on the Rock: A Rebel Returns to His Faith* (e3press, 2000). He was brought up in a traditional Catholic family but left the church in adolescence because he found so little that was relevant to his life. He found a spiritual home briefly in several Protestant denominations, but then founded his own independent church: New Covenant Fellowship. For a while it was a thriving community, but then serious divisions arose that eventually split the church. Cavins himself suffered personally through this ordeal. As he says, half of the church elders supported him while the other half sided with the discontented members. Being an independent church, there was no ecclesial structure or body with authority to mediate the dispute or make some decision. The community had always prided itself on its independence. But now, as Cavins says, "There remained a real sense of isolation and unconnectedness from the historical church."

Ironically, New Covenant Fellowship had labored hard to root itself in the Jewish scriptures and traditions, but it now found itself unconnected to its *Christian* roots. They were unfamiliar with any other independent church or with any church that had existed for the past 2000 years. In fact, Cavins says, "We didn't even know what the rest of the believing church believed.... We'd set out to build the new Jerusalem; we'd ended up with a badly wounded little church in Ohio and a pastor who wasn't sure what he believed, why he believed it, and whether he had the authority to be a pastor at all." So he resigned his pastorate, continued his spiritual search, and ended up rejoining the church of his youth. Like Scott Hahn, Jeff Cavins now exercises a dynamic teaching ministry within the Catholic Church.

One more example is Alex Jones, pastor of a small but vibrant African-American Pentecostal church in Detroit. One day he was inspired to promise the congregation to celebrate a worship service modeled on that of the early Christian church. But as he began researching documents for this purpose, he discovered some things he wasn't prepared for. He found, for example, that the early church service was not free-flowing. It had a definite structure. Not only did it include song, prayer, Bible reading and preaching, but it also had a sacramental dimension—an offering of bread and wine, a consecratory prayer, and a communion service.

As he studied further, Jones found there was also a hierarchical dimension to the service: a presiding bishop or priest, a deacon, and ministers of the Eucharist as well as the participating faithful. He read more and more about the history of the early church, including the patristic writings (the so-called "Fathers of the Church"). He began to think: The true church of Jesus Christ must be the one that is closest to the time of the apostles. Which church would that be? It could not be his own since it was only a few years old. The Baptist church, indeed all the Protestant churches, went back no further than the sixteenth century. Could it be—no, surely not the Catholic Church! He had always been taught to abhor that corrupt institution. Yet the more he studied and prayed, the more convinced he became. But how could he abandon his congregation? How would he support his family? After sleepless nights he finally decided: I must be obedient to where the Lord is leading me. Thankfully, his family accepted his decision and became Catholic along with him, together with about sixty members of his congregation. He tells the whole story in the video *No Price Too High* (St. Joseph Communications, 2001).

❖ ❖ ❖

Church and Tradition

For many people, one of the most attractive features of the Catholic Church is the fact that it is rooted in history. The church claims to have been founded by Christ himself and is able to trace itself back to the time of the first apostles. This apostolic origin is often regarded as one of the four "marks" or signs whereby the true church of Christ can be recognized. Churches that were founded later in history agree that the Catholic Church was the original Christian church but that it became corrupt over time, lost or changed some of the essential teachings of the Bible, and therefore needed to be radically re-formed. The Catholic Church, on the other hand, claims that it is constantly guided by the Holy Spirit in such a way that it will never lose or change what belongs to the substance of divine revelation, though it may fall into error or defection on matters that are peripheral but not substantive.

One of the main dividing points between Catholic and Protestant churches involves the question: What is the *source* of divine revelation? How do we know what God has revealed and what we are to believe in order to attain salvation? Since the time of Martin Luther, the classic Protestant answer has been "the Bible alone" (*Sola Scriptura* in Latin). Whereas the Catholic answer is the Bible as understood through the ongoing, living *Tradition* of the church. (I will use "Tradition" whenever referring to the central content of church teaching and "tradition(s)" to designate particular cultural or time-bound beliefs and practices that may change, such as the various languages and postures used during Mass, the practice of fasting, public processions, and the like).

33

It is not that Scripture and Tradition are two *separate* sources of divine truth. The Second Vatican Council taught that together both form "one sacred deposit of the Word of God," which is entrusted to the teaching authority of the church (*Constitution on Divine Revelation*, n. 10). In other words, the Bible alone, without the guidance of Tradition, is not a complete guide to God's revealed truth. This is because the meaning of biblical passages is not always self-evident. Interestingly, the phrase "the Bible alone" is found nowhere in the Bible itself. On the contrary, the need for guidance in understanding it is expressed in the Bible. When the Ethiopian official in his chariot was reading the words of the prophet Isaiah, Philip the deacon asked him, "Do you understand what you are reading?" The man replied, "How can I, unless someone guides me?" (Acts 8:30-31). Moreover, one of the letters of Peter warns against the danger of distorting the biblical texts. Speaking of Paul's letters he says, "There are some things in them hard to understand, which the ignorant and unstable twist to their own destruction, as they do the other scriptures" (2 Peter 3:16). At the same time, the notion of Tradition is found already in the Bible. Saint Paul writes: "So then, brothers and sisters, stand firm and hold fast to the traditions that you were taught by us, either by word of mouth or by our letter" (2 Thessalonians 2:15). Also, in writing to Timothy, bishop of Ephesus, Paul says "...what you have heard from me through many witnesses, entrust to faithful people who will be able to teach others as well" (2 Timothy 2:2).

> *The Bible alone, without the guidance of Tradition, is not a complete guide to God's revealed truth.*

❖ ❖ ❖

Tradition and the Bible

So it is clear that from the earliest apostolic times Christian believers were instructed not by the reading of books (most were unable to read and books were rare) but by teachers who themselves had absorbed the Tradition of the living church. Tradition is simply the set of beliefs held by the Christian community and handed down by word of mouth from one generation to the next. An important truth often forgotten by Catholics and Protestants alike is that the community we call "the church" was in existence long before the book we know as the Bible came to be.

Which leads to an interesting question: How, then, was the Bible formed? First, it is crucial to remember that we learn who God is through the stories of God's *actions* in human history: creation, the call of Abraham, the Exodus, the covenant between God and the Jews, the preaching of the prophets, and the exile and homecoming of God's people. Long before these events were written down, people remembered these wonderful deeds of God and orally recounted them for their children. Eventually, various authors wrote them down, under divine inspiration, so that there would be no substantial errors.

The same basic pattern followed for the New Testament writings. The stories about the life and teachings of Jesus were passed on by word of mouth. In fact, there was no written "gospel" until at least three decades after Jesus' resurrection. Luke, who wrote his gospel around 80-85 A.D., clearly says in his prologue that his material was "handed on" to him by "eyewitnesses and servants of the word" (1:2). By this time the letters of Paul, John and Peter were also circulating among

35

the Christians.

The problem was that many other writings—some of them quite popular and inspirational—were also becoming common. These have become known as the "apocryphal" writings: the Gospel of Thomas, the Gospel of Peter, and the Gospel of the Egyptians. Eventually, the question had to be addressed: Which of these writings are inspired (and therefore Scripture) and which are not? Remember, there was no Bible as yet. It had not even been decided which of the Old Testament writings were to be regarded as inspired.

Who had the authority to decide such important questions? History gives us the answer: It was the community, especially the elders (presbyters and bishops), who would gather in councils to prayerfully discern which writings were in harmony with the oral Tradition that had been handed on from generation to generation. Both Protestants and Catholics believe that the church community was guided by the Holy Spirit in these decisions. It was not till the end of the fourth century (392) that church councils gave final approval to the present books of the Bible. This could raise troubling questions for some Protestant Christians, especially Fundamentalists: If the Bible is the sole guide for faith and salvation, how could people believe and be saved before there was a Bible? Catholics believe that since the Bible (as a book) grew out of the believing community under the inspiration of the Holy Spirit, it must be read and interpreted with the help of the community.

Catholics are sometimes criticized for ignoring the Bible and placing too much faith in their sacraments, devotions and rituals. There may have been some truth to this charge in the past when Catholics were not given much encouragement to read the Bible. But today this is no longer valid. The Second Vatican Council insists that "like the Christian religion itself, all the preaching of the church must be nourished and ruled by Sacred Scripture" (*Constitution on Divine Revelation,* n. 21). This is why every time we gather for worship—whether for Mass, the sacraments, or devotions—the church gives a prominent place to the reading of God's word.

Moreover, in n. 25 of the same document from the Council, individual Catholics are encouraged to read the Scriptures: "This sacred Synod earnestly and specifically urges all the Christian faithful...to learn by frequent reading of the divine Scriptures the 'excelling knowledge of Jesus Christ'" (Philippians 3:8). The Council quotes Saint Jerome: "Ignorance of the Scriptures is ignorance of Christ." The Council also reminds us that our reading of Scripture should always be accompanied by prayer.

I like what theologian Alan Schreck says in his book *Catholic and Christian* (Servant Books, 1984): The Bible cannot be separated from Tradition or from the teaching authority of the popes and bishops. In the early church, as we have seen, all three "grew up" together.

Growth of the Early Church

Historians generally are amazed at the rapid spread of Christianity, even in the first decades after Christ's death. Christian communities could be found in cities like Antioch in Syria; Ephesus, Miletus and Smyrna in Asia Minor (present-day Turkey); Athens, Corinth, Thessalonica and Philippi in Greece; Pozzuoli and Rome in Italy. In the second century, it spread to cities in France such as Vienne and Lyons, and into Spain. As William Bausch states in his *Pilgrim Church* (Twenty-Third Publications, 1989), "the network of church-communities in the first two centuries spanned from Spain to Germany and from Yugoslavia of today to the Black Sea" (p. 22). The church took root in northern Africa in the first century. Its chief city, Alexandria, had a major role in the early church. It was at the crossroads of Greco-Roman civilization and so provided an opportunity for the gospel to encounter the dominant culture. For many years, Alexandria in Egypt and Antioch in Syria became the centers of Christian theological reflection and writing.

There were a number of reasons for the rapid spread of Christianity. Foremost was the missionary spirit of the first Christians. They took seriously "the Great Commission" of Jesus to carry his gospel message "to all the nations" (Matthew 28:19; Mark 16:15). The task of evangelizing was not limited to the bishops and presbyters; the laity understood their baptismal commitment to include the mission to witness to their faith in Jesus both by word and example.

We can imagine the process going something like this: The new Christian converts, whether from Judaism or paganism, lived their newfound faith—not in an ostentatious manner, but in a way that was genuine and convincing. Their Jewish and Gentile neighbors observed how the Christians were devoted to their families, were conscientious in their jobs, did not go along with the immoral sexual practices of the time, and reached out in care to those who were poor or sick. Moreover, they did all this with a spirit of joy and peacefulness. At some point the Jew or Gentile would say, "You know, you've changed. What's happened to you?" And the Christian would say, "You're right—I've come to know Jesus Christ, and it's made all the difference." "Well, tell me about him." And the Christian would proceed to tell the story of Jesus. If the other person was ready, he or she would say, "That's what I'm looking for. What do I need to do?" The Christian would then connect the person to the community and eventually to the catechumenate. Later when the persecutions began, many pagans were impressed by the courage of the Christian martyrs who were willing to endure torture and even death for their belief in Christ. As the ancient Christian writer Tertullian put it: "The blood of martyrs is the seed of the church."

William Bausch cites another interesting reason for the spread of the early church: the strong sense of bonding and communion among the Christians. He quotes extensively from an agnostic writer, E.R. Dodds, who believes that the church was highly visible as a caring community. It took care of widows and orphans, the old, the unemployed, and the disabled. It provided a burial fund for the poor and a nursing service in the event of plague or disease. But even more important was the sense of belonging that people found in the Christian community. They truly cared about one another. They saw themselves as "members one of another." In Dodds' view, this was probably the strongest single cause for the spread of Christianity. Bausch concludes, "Fraternal love, it seems, was the most powerful force."

> *When the persecutions began, many pagans were impressed by the courage of the Christian martyrs.*

❖ ❖ ❖

Dissensions and Persecutions

It is always tempting to idealize "the early church" as some kind of pure paradise from which the church fell, never again to recover. But the truth is that tensions and controversies marked the Christian church from the very beginning. In his two letters to the Corinthians, Saint Paul sternly rebuked the members of that church for their infighting, their factions, and their laissez-faire tolerance of moral laxity. The Letter of James scolded his local church for favoring the wealthy and marginalizing the poor. Modern biblical scholars have shown that even the gospel accounts of Jesus' words and actions were selected with a view toward settling disputes going on in the various Christian communities. The early church was no utopia of Christianity.

The Acts of the Apostles shows the early church dealing with at least two thorny issues. One was the question of whether the disciples of Jesus were to remain as a sect within Judaism or to separate and form a distinct religious community as the messianic fulfillment of Judaism. Closely related was the question of whether the Gentile converts should be obliged to undergo circumcision and be bound by Mosaic Law. There were good people on both sides. To settle the matter, the apostles and elders met in Jerusalem in what has sometimes been called the first general council of the church. After much debate, the views of Paul and Silas prevailed. The "new covenant" inaugurated by Jesus, while in continuity with the former covenant, was to embrace both Jews and Gentiles, indeed all humanity, in a universal community no longer identified with Judaism exclusively. Therefore, Gentile converts who accepted baptism were not bound to circumcision or the Law of Moses, except for a few minor dietary observances (Acts 15:1-29). The main point for our purposes is that the early church was not free of problems and dissensions but the members did not deny or ignore them. Rather they were free to bring them into the open and reflect on them in the light of what Jesus had tried to teach them. They believed that in doing so they were being guided by the Holy Spirit, whom Jesus had promised would guide them to truth (John 16:13).

The other obstacle the church had to face in its early years was persecution. We read in Acts that "a severe persecution broke out against the church in Jerusalem" within a short time after Pentecost (8:1). This persecution was inaugurated by some Jewish leaders after the death of Stephen, the first Christian martyr, and spread even into Syria through the zeal of the young rabbi Saul of Tarsus, the future Saint Paul. This persecution apparently did not last long, but one positive effect was that many Christians who had to flee Jerusalem brought the gospel message to more distant places, such as Phoenicia, Cyprus and Antioch (Acts 11:19).

The most sustained persecutions, however, were those carried out by the Roman Empire. They were not constant. Some emperors were more tolerant than others of the Christian religion, but Rome was generally suspicious of any new sect or cult, fearing the potential for rebellion. As a matter of law, Christians could be accused of atheism, insofar as they denied the reality and power of the pagan gods. The atheism charge also included subversion, since the state looked upon its official religion as a strong cohesive force for the empire. Indeed, it was not difficult to know who the Christians were.

As William Bausch says, they would not buy meat that had been offered to idols. A Christian jeweler would not decorate a pagan statue. Christians would not attend the gladiator contests and would not serve in the army since they were pacifists. They shunned luxuries because they wanted to follow Christ more fully. Because they were so different, Saint Justin Martyr wrote, the very name "Christian" became associated with suspicions of every kind.

We can only imagine the sense of anxiety under which these Christians had to conduct their lives day after day.

The first Roman persecution began in 64 A.D. with the emperor Nero, when a terrible fire destroyed more than half of Rome. Nero blamed the Christians, though theories differ on who actually started the fire and some even point to Nero himself as the cause of it. Both Peter and Paul were martyred at this time, together with a long list of Christians whose names and deeds later filled the books of the early Christian communities. Other persecutions broke out under the emperors Domitian, Trajan, Hadrian, Marcus Aurelius, and others. Bausch notes that in 303 the emperor Diocletian issued a severe decree against Christians, calling for the destruction of all Christian places and instruments of worship, loss of rank among the nobility, and a general loss of legal rights for all Christians. We can only imagine the sense of anxiety under which these Christians had to conduct their lives day after day, never knowing when they or their loved ones would be reduced to poverty, imprisoned, or killed. It is a profound tribute to their faith that so many refused to deny their belief in

Christ in order to save their own lives. They must have meditated often on the words of Jesus: "For those who want to save their life will lose it, and those who lose their life for my sake will find it" (Matthew 16:25).

Finally, in the year 311, the emperor Galerius issued an edict of toleration toward Christians. A few years later, under the emperor Constantine, Christianity was granted full freedom of worship. Christians could now emerge from hiding and even build their own churches. The era of persecution was over except for a brief revival under Julian (361-363), who was later dubbed "the Apostate." As tragic as the years of persecution were, they remain important formative periods in the history of the church. In our liturgies today we continue to remember with gratitude the martyrs who remained faithful to their profession and inspired faith in the hearts of generations to come.

The Christian Empire

In the year 381, a remarkable event occurred in the history of the church. The emperor Theodosius I, a Christian, decreed that Christianity would henceforth be the official religion of the Roman Empire. Only a few years later (392), paganism was outlawed. The empire had now come full circle. Non-Christians were now the outlaws, and Christians were the privileged class.

This development turned out to be a mixed blessing for the church. On the positive side, it made Christianity respectable as well as safe. No longer did Christians have to fear for their property or their lives. Beautiful basilicas, decorated with rich mosaics, were built for worship. Artists depicted the images of Jesus, Mary and the saints in brilliantly colored icons. Thousands of people came seeking baptism and entrance into the Christian community. Having just emerged from some 250 years of persecution, Christians tended to look upon Constantine, Theodosius and the empire as their champions.

At the same time, something was lost in this transition. For one thing, the church and the civil government were too closely tied. Bishops and priests were reluctant to speak out against the opulence of the imperial court and the government's neglect of the poor and suffering. Christians themselves could become too comfortable with the status quo. Courageous preachers like Saint John Chrysostom, bishop of Constantinople, the new capital of the empire, was one who spoke out against the luxury and frivolous lifestyles of the court rulers. He also challenged the ordinary faithful on their tendency to ignore the poor citizens of the empire: "How can you clothe the body of Christ with silver and gold on the altar," he would say, "but neglect the body of Christ shivering in your streets?"

Another problem was that those entering the church often did so not out of conviction but out of convenience. Once paganism was outlawed, many of those asking for baptism were Christian in name only, with no serious intention of conforming their lives to the values of Christ. The result, as one writer put it, was that "the spiritual and moral fervor of the church inevitably waned." The ranks of the church were swelled with weakly committed Christians enjoying the blessings of imperial favor.

One positive outgrowth of this phenomenon was the

development of the monastic life. Some Christians, convinced that they could not truly follow Christ in the midst of such a world, retired to the desert or other remote places to seek "the one thing necessary." Some, both men and women, did so as solitary hermits. Others gathered in communities for mutual support and communal prayer. Gradually, these movements were institutionalized by way of written rules and a daily regimen of prayer, study and manual labor. The faithful would often seek out the spiritual guidance of these "athletes of Christ" rather than their own parish clergy, whom they perceived to be too preoccupied with worldly matters. Of course, it was not only the monks and hermits who embodied Christian holiness in these imperial times. There were a good number of clergy and laity who lived their faith generously in the midst of a material culture.

Other Struggles

Meanwhile, other dark clouds were gathering on the horizon. Not all the inhabitants of the Roman Empire were cultured and civilized. Particularly in the West—Germany, France, Spain and Britain—there were numerous rustic people that were commonly known as "barbarians." They were kept in check as long as the Roman army remained strong. But the empire was beginning to decline, both militarily and culturally. Since the center of the empire was now in the East (Constantinople), Rome was left without a strong leader. Eventually, the barbarians swept into Italy and the unthinkable happened: the Visigoth leader Alaric sacked the city of Rome for the first time in 700 years. Many thought civilization itself had come to an end.

Just fifty years later, Attila the Hun led his warriors into Italy. By this time the strongest person in Rome was its bishop, Pope Leo I. He went out personally to meet Attila and talked him into sparing the city in exchange for an annual payment of tribute. But the barbarians continued to overrun France, Britain and Africa. Finally in 476, the Ostrogoths invaded Italy, deposed the ruler, and declared one of their own as king of Italy. This date is generally regarded as the fall of the Western Roman Empire.

The Eastern Roman Empire remained generally peaceful. In fact, the emperor Justinian in 529 attacked the barbarians and succeeded in reuniting the empire for a short time. He celebrated his victories by building the magnificent Hagia Sophia in Constantinople. One of the impressive mosaics there depicts Constantine on one side presenting the city of Constantinople to Christ and Justinian on the other presenting the new basilica to him.

Less than a century later, however, another threat to Christendom arose. Out of Persia and Arabia, Muslim armies swept through the Christian lands of Syria, Palestine and Egypt, determined to impose their new religion on the inhabitants. In a short time, Christianity in these regions withered away, including the once-great centers of Jerusalem, Antioch and Alexandria. Next the Muslims invaded Africa and crossed over into Europe by way of Spain. They even attacked Constantinople but were unable to take it. It was not until 1453 that the great city fell—sacked, ironically, by so-called Christian crusaders in the Fourth Crusade.

The church remained a symbol of strength through all these turbulent times. In the West, at least, it was the one institution that provided stability and continuity. By and large, the bishops were well-educated and skilled administrators. They filled a power vacuum left by civil servants who were unable to govern. Moreover, the missionaries took upon themselves the task of evangelizing the barbarian peoples, most of whom had an appreciation of Roman culture and organization and were not overly difficult to convert. They saw the church as the repository of moral authority, learning and culture. They looked to the bishops more than to secular kings as the leaders of society.

They saw the church as the repository of moral authority, learning and culture.

Another stabilizing influence when civil governments collapsed was the rise of monasticism, particularly the Benedictine tradition. The Rule of Saint Benedict provided its adherents with a well-ordered and balanced spiritual life that attracted many, especially among the educated classes. From the fifth through the seventh centuries, hundreds of these monasteries sprang up throughout Europe. To them must be given much of the credit for preserving learning and culture through the so-called Dark Ages. As William Bausch notes: "They did not start out with the intention of preserving and passing on culture, but that is what they did. In establishing their houses, these upper-class men began to clear forests, reclaim land, and give some system to agriculture. In so doing, they were laying the foundations for economic recovery and stability. In addition, the monks began copying manuscripts so that nothing of the glorious past was lost."

One of the most famous of these monks was the one who

became bishop of Rome in 590 and took the name Gregory I (called "the Great"). As pope he combined monastic holiness with missionary zeal and genius for organization. One of his most notable achievements was to send the Benedictine monk Augustine to evangelize England. He converted the king, Ethelbert, and established his see at Canterbury, becoming the first Catholic bishop of England. Some years later the English Catholics sent their own missionaries, led by Saint Boniface, back to the mainland. This tireless evangelist brought about the conversion of the German peoples and thus established Christianity and the church in the heart of Europe.

My purpose in laying out this brief history of early Christianity is twofold. First, I want to show that the Catholic Church of today is rooted in the first-century Christian community of the apostles and the generations immediately following. To be sure, the shape and the dynamics of the church have evolved a great deal over the years, but the basic outlines, the core beliefs and values are very similar. Second, I want to highlight the truth that from the very beginning the church has been troubled both by external stresses and by internal dissensions. It had to endure the persecutions, deal with the barbarian invasions, resist the Muslim conquests, and work through its own power struggles. (We have passed over the fierce doctrinal controversies that racked the church in these first centuries, but we will consider them in a later chapter.) I think most readers will agree: This dynamic and vast church history offers contemporary Catholics a wealth of experience and tradition from which to draw guidance.

Reason #3

Sacraments

Ways We Meet Christ

One of the distinctive features of Catholicism is that it is a sacramental religion. It believes that God can be encountered not only in the Sacred Scriptures and in nature, but also in certain ritual actions. Many older Catholics can recite the old catechism definition of a sacrament as "an outward sign instituted by Jesus Christ to give grace." While this is not an erroneous definition, it begs for explanation.

One of the earliest heresies the church had to confront was the notion that the visible, material world was evil. Manicheans, Gnostics, and other groups held to a dualistic concept of reality borrowed from Greek philosophy: spirit was good; matter was evil. Against this notion the early church theologians insisted that the material world, the world of nature, came from the creative hand of God and was therefore good. Indeed, the visible creation can reveal the invisible presence of God. The Psalms of the Bible are filled with poetic expressions of this truth: "The heavens are telling the glory of God, and the firmament proclaims his handiwork" (Psalms 19:1). According to Saint Paul, even people without faith are capable of knowing something of God by reflecting on the beauty, order and harmony of the visible creation: "For what can be known about God is plain to them.... Ever since the creation of the world his eternal power and divine nature, invisible though they are, have been understood and seen through the things he has made" (Romans 1:19-20).

Contemporary theologians call this "the sacramental principle;" that is, the visible, material world reveals the presence of invisible, spiritual realities. Ordinarily, we humans do not have direct access to these realities. The exception would be the mystics who sometimes have a direct experience of God, Jesus, Mary, angels, and the like. But ordinarily, because we ourselves are both body and spirit, we need to see, hear and touch material reality in order to know the spiritual.

This is why the Incarnation of the Son of God is such a key mystery for Christians. By entering our world in human form, Jesus reveals God to us. If we want to know what God is like, we need only contemplate the words and actions of Jesus. When one of Jesus' disciples begged him to "show us the Father, and we will be satisfied," Jesus answered, "Have I been with you all this time, Philip, and you still do not know me? Whoever has seen me has seen the Father" (John 14:8-9). So, as theologians like to say, Jesus himself is "the original sacrament," the holy presence of God embodied before our eyes. As we say in the Preface of the Mass for Christmas, "In him we see our God made visible, and so are caught up in the love of the God we cannot see."

So far most Christians would have no difficulty accepting this line of thinking. The Catholic Church, however, takes the sacramental principles one step further. As reported in the Acts of the Apostles, Paul, who at this point was still calling himself Saul, was traveling to Damascus in order to arrest and imprison the Christian converts there. On the way he was struck to the ground by a blinding light and heard a voice say, "Saul, Saul, why do you persecute me?" "Who are you?" Saul asked. And the voice replied, "I am Jesus, whom you are persecuting" (Acts 9:4-5). As the story continues, Saul becomes convinced that Christ is truly risen from the dead, that the Christian religion is the true fulfillment of Judaism, and that he must become one of them. But another truth was deeply impressed on his mind: In persecuting the Christians, he was in reality persecuting Christ. In other words, Christ was somehow, mystically but really, present in the Christian community. Later on he began using the vivid image of the church as "the body of Christ" (1 Corinthians 12:27; Ephesians 1:22-23; Colossians 1:18). Just as Christ is the sacrament (the visible sign) of God, so the church is the sacrament of Christ. This is admittedly bold language, but in essence it is no different from what Jesus himself says in the gospels. In describing the Last Judgment, he awards eternal life to those who think beyond themselves to care for the poor and needy and condemns those who did not: "Truly I tell you, just as you did it to one of the least of these who are members of my family, you did it to me" (Matthew 25:40). To touch the members of Christ's body, whether for good or for ill, is to touch Christ himself.

The other application of the sacramental principle involves the sacraments themselves. One good way to understand the sacraments is to view them as actions, the actions of Christ extended in space and time. During his days on earth, Jesus forgave sins, brought healing to sick people, changed bread and wine into his body and blood for our spiritual nourishment, and commissioned the apostles to do the same in his memory. Over time the church reflected on these actions and concluded that Jesus had left behind seven special actions or signs wherein the faithful could encounter the risen Christ and receive spiritual help for their pilgrimage on earth. As Saint Augustine put it in one of his memorable homilies: When the church baptizes, it is Christ who baptizes—and likewise confirms, forgives sins, becomes present in the Eucharist, anoints for healing, joins a couple together in sacred marriage, and ordains ministers for service in the church. There was never a doubt that Christ also meets us through his word in Scripture and in the person of our brothers and sisters. But the sacraments are seen as privileged moments when we are touched by Christ with special graces for times of need in our spiritual journey.

Baptism

This is the foundational sacrament of initiation into the divine life that Jesus came to bring us and into the Christian community where that life will be further nurtured. The Acts of the Apostles makes the primacy of this sacrament especially clear. On Pentecost Sunday the apostles "were filled with the Holy Spirit and began to speak" (2:4). Peter gave an extended homily in which he interpreted the event for his fellow Jews in the light of the Old Testament prophecies. When he had finished, the crowd asked, "Brothers, what should we do?" Peter replied, "Repent and be baptized, every one of you, in the name of Jesus Christ, so that your sins may be forgiven" (2:37-38). The text concludes by noting that about 3000 people were baptized and added to the community that day. The apostles were acting upon "the Great Commission" that Jesus had given them at his ascension into heaven: "Go therefore and make disciples of all nations, baptizing them in the name of the Father, and of the Son, and of the Holy Spirit" (Matthew 28:19). References to baptism continue through Acts as well as in the letters of Peter and Paul.

What is the significance of baptism? We can gain some insight just by reflecting on the ritual itself. The baptized are washed with water, an obvious symbol for some sort of cleansing. What is being cleansed or washed away is sin. The ritual presupposes that the (adult) person has come to know Jesus Christ, wants to belong to him and to the Christian community, and desires to live a holy life in conformity with the examples and teachings of Jesus. This calls for repentance, a break with one's past patterns of sin and self-indulgence. In the early church the new converts would step down into a pool of water, be immersed three times, walk up the other steps, and then be clothed with a white robe. Meaning: they left their past, sinful lives behind in the waters and were "reborn" as disciples of Christ, called to a new life of holiness. Baptisms typically took place at the Easter Vigil in the presence of the whole community, and the new converts wore their white robes till the following Sunday. In recent years the church has been trying to reclaim some of this dramatic ritual through the Rite of Christian Initiation of Adults (RCIA). The candidates for baptism go through a

Baptisms typically took place at the Easter Vigil in the presence of the whole community.

lengthy period of instruction, are presented to the parish community during the Sundays of Lent, and then are baptized at the Easter Vigil, sometimes by immersion as described above.

Another gift of baptism is the profound transformation that takes place in the depths of the soul. The newly baptized are given the incomparable dignity of being the beloved daughters and sons of God. Recall for a moment the baptism of Jesus. This is one of the very few times where an incident in the life of Christ is recorded by all four gospel writers—an indication of the importance given to it by the Christian community. The text says, "...the heaven was opened, and the Holy Spirit descended upon him in bodily form like a dove. And a voice came from heaven, 'You are my Son, the Beloved; with you I am well pleased'" (Luke 3:21-22). Here we have the revelation of the true identity of Jesus of Nazareth. He is not just "the carpenter's son," the child of Mary and Joseph, the day laborer, or the teacher with wise sayings. He is the beloved Son of God.

Now, following the sacramental principle, we have to say that what happened to Jesus at his baptism is also revealed and reproduced in us. God the Father gazes upon us with the look of love and says, "You are now my beloved son or daughter; with you I am well pleased." Baptism joins us, invisibly but truly, to Jesus Christ. "I am the vine, you are the branches," he says. "Abide in me as I abide in you" (John 15:4-5). Or, to use Paul's image, we are the body of Christ, joined to him as our head. Therefore, we are the beloved of God, just as he is.

If we could truly believe that truth, what a profound sense of dignity it could give us. It could free us from those nagging thoughts that keep us doubting our self-worth. Henri Nouwen, in his beautiful book *Life of the Beloved* (Crossroad, 1992), says that self-rejection "is the greatest enemy of the spiritual life because it contradicts the sacred voice that calls us 'the Beloved.' Being the Beloved expresses the core truth of our existence." The trouble, he says, is that we tend to pay too much attention to those other, louder voices that keep telling us, "Prove that you are worth something; do something relevant, spectacular or powerful, and then you will earn the love you so desire." Instead, we need to listen to that softer voice that keeps gently reminding us who we truly are: the beloved of God. This, by the way, is the basic meaning of the word "grace." Grace is the free, unearned gift of God's unconditional love poured into our soul at baptism.

I will never forget the Easter Vigil service I attended some years ago at a Catholic college campus. Four of the students were baptized that night. The church was packed with people, and the choir and ministers conducted the service with great care. When it came time for the baptism, one by one the students stepped into the water and were immersed in it. When they came out, the choir burst into a beautiful song: "You Are God's Work of Art." I was deeply moved by this wonderful expression of the truth: "You are the beloved of God."

So far we have been talking about adult baptism. Most of us, though, are more familiar with infant baptism. Sometimes Catholics are challenged on this point by evangelical Christians: Baptism should not be conferred until one can make a free choice to become a Christian, they say, and besides, infant baptism is not in Scripture. While it is true that the first Christians were adults, infant baptism is nowhere denied in Scripture. In fact, at least in a couple of places it is implied.

Saint Paul says he baptized "the household of Stephanas" (1 Corinthians 1:16). In Acts we read that he baptized the new convert Lydia and "her household" (16:15), as well as the prison jailer "and his entire family" (16:33). Presumably, there were some minor children in these three families.

By the second century, Christian families were bringing their little children to the church for baptism.

Here again, though, we do well to attend to the history and practice of the church. By the second century, Christian families were bringing their little children to the church for baptism. They wanted their children to be joined to Christ and the church from the beginning of their young lives. The parents pledged themselves to instruct the children in the faith and to model Christian living for them. One of the early witnesses to the practice of infant baptism is the *Apostolic Tradition*, a document written by Saint Hippolytus around the year 220. He describes the process of preparation for baptism and the rite of conferral. Little children were baptized first, answering the questions of intent for themselves if they could; otherwise, the parents or family members would answer for them, much as we do today when parents bring their infants for baptism.

With infant baptism, of course, there is no repentance, since infants are incapable of personal sin. But church teaching is that baptism frees them from "original sin." This has been viewed as a state of alienation from God that is passed on to every human from the "original" sin of Adam and Eve in Paradise. Nowadays most theologians are rethinking this concept, but the core truth here is that each of us enters this world as a blend of spiritual light and darkness. On the one hand, we are created "in the image and likeness of God" (Genesis 1:26) with a basic goodness that orients us toward God as our final end.

At the same time, however, we find within ourselves an opposite tendency toward self-gratification and self-glorification. Left unchecked, this tendency can propel us toward choices that are evil and destructive. Saint Paul described this struggle vividly in his Letter to the Romans (7:14-25). Our human nature is good but wounded. We are in need of some kind of supernatural help to move us toward the good and away from evil. Baptism supplies this supernatural "grace" for infants. While not entirely obliterating sinful tendencies, baptism roots us in a power greater than ourselves—won for us by the death and resurrection of Christ—and joins us to him in the depths of our being. But that relationship needs to be constantly tended and nurtured. That is the function of prayer, the other sacraments, and the teaching and example of devoted parents. I have always thought that infant baptism is a wonderful way to proclaim the truth that we are not made holy and righteous by our own efforts. That is a free gift of God. Before an infant has done anything to "deserve" it, God gazes upon that child with infinite love and says, "You are my beloved; in you I am well pleased."

There are two other effects of baptism that we need to consider. For one, whether adult or infant, the baptized person is given a set of spiritual powers called "virtues," the main ones being faith, hope and charity. These give the ability to believe in God and in the truths of the Christian faith, to have confidence that God will give us everything we need to help us reach eternal life, and to have the capacity to love

God and love our neighbor even when it is difficult to do so. These are wondrous gifts indeed. So much in the world around us can tempt us to lose faith, doubt the goodness of God, distrust one another, or live for ourselves rather than care about others. The supernatural virtues serve to heal us of these negative tendencies. But again, they require nurturing, especially through prayer and the reading of Scripture.

The other effect of baptism, which has not always been appreciated by Catholics, is that it commits us to some form of service or ministry. When priests and nuns were numerous, Catholics took it for granted that they would carry on the church's ministries. But again, that was not the case in earlier church history. The New Testament letters are filled with references to the variety of gifts present in the ordinary faithful, together with exhortations to make use of these gifts to build up the church community. One example from Saint Paul: "For as in one body we have many members, and not all the members have the same function, so we who are many are one body in Christ, and individually we are members of one another. We have gifts that differ according to the grace given to us." Then he goes on to mention the variety of gifts: prophecy, service, teaching, exhortation, generosity, leadership and compassion (Romans 12:4-8). Note that these are not attributed just to those who hold office in the church; they are presumed to be distributed by the Holy Spirit to all the faithful in their baptism. Nowadays the church is growing increasingly aware that each member of the community has some gift(s) to share, whether for the parish or for the wider community. Another name for this is "stewardship."

Confirmation

There is some confusion among Catholics today about the sacrament of confirmation, mainly because the time for its conferral seems to keep changing. When I was in school we were confirmed in fifth or sixth grade. Then for many years the sacrament was given in late high school. Nowadays it can be given to either adolescents or preadolescents, depending on the bishop of the diocese.

The basic reason for this disparity can be traced back to the early church—there were two interpretations of confirmation operating in different parts of the Christian world and at different times. One interpretation understands confirmation as a "sacrament of initiation" that is conferred immediately after (or soon after) baptism, making the person a full member of the church and "sealing" him or her with the gifts of the Holy Spirit. The other interpretation sees confirmation as a "sacrament of strengthening" that should be given when the person is growing up and in need of special graces to live the Christian life in the face of temptations. In general, the Eastern churches have followed the first interpretation while in the West, including the United States, the second has prevailed. The fact is, both theologies are valid and recognized by the church's teaching authority.

Perhaps the best way to understand confirmation is to view it through its effects. *The Catechism of the Catholic Church* states that the sacrament deepens and strengthens the grace of baptism, rooting us more firmly in our relationship with Christ and the church. But most of all, it is a "special outpouring of the Holy Spirit as once granted to the apostles on the day of Pentecost" (n. 1302). It is clear from Acts that the apostles and the other missionaries used the practice of "laying on of hands" and/or "anointing with oil," either at the time of baptism or later. Either way, the effect was the same: an outpouring of the Holy Spirit (Acts 8:14-17; 10:44-48; 19:1-7).

To understand confirmation we must first understand the role of the Holy Spirit in our lives. Earlier we saw that baptism confers on us that wonderful dignity of being beloved sons and daughters of God the Father, as well as brothers and sisters of the Lord Jesus. But we also are given a special relationship with the Holy Spirit: We become the living "dwelling place" of the Spirit. Jesus promised the disciples at the Last Supper: "I will ask the Father, and he will give you another Advocate to be with you forever. This is the Spirit of truth, whom the world cannot receive, because it neither sees him nor knows him. But you know him, because he abides with you, and he will be within you" (John 14:16-17). That promise was fulfilled at Pentecost when the Spirit descended upon the disciples with a mighty show of power. The gift of the Spirit was not intended for them alone but for all subsequent believers. When Paul urged the community at Corinth to avoid sins against chastity, he gave them a profound reason: "Do you not know that your body is a temple of the Holy Spirit within you, which you have from God...?" (1 Corinthians 6:19). This image of our body as a sacred temple of the Holy Spirit can be a powerful motive not only for chastity but also for cultivating a sense of reverence for our own body and that of others. How can we inflict physical harm or violence, sexual abuse, or verbal insults on those in whom the Holy Spirit dwells?

Speaking of decisions leads us to another important role for the Holy Spirit: to give us courage, or "the gift of fortitude." Fear and anxiety are "hardwired" in our nervous system. They arise spontaneously whenever we perceive danger or threat—not only physical harm but also psychological hurt. We are often afraid of failing, of being rejected, of being humiliated, or of losing something or someone dear to us. Such fears are natural and normal. They arise from the simple fact that we are human, we are limited, and we don't have total control over our environment or over other people. So when the Bible says "Do not be afraid," it cannot mean "Never feel any fear." That would be inhuman. Instead, feel your fear, but do not let fear determine your choices. Do not let it drive you to actions that are unworthy of you as a Christian. Do the right thing, do the loving thing—in spite of your fears.

If we think about it, a good number of sins are committed out of fear rather than malice. People tell lies because they fear the truth will get them into trouble. Young people (and even the not-so-young) go along with un-Christian behaviors because they fear not being accepted by their peers. Some people agree to non-marital sex out of fear of losing their partner. So the Holy Spirit, with the gift of fortitude, gives us the courage to stand firm in our convictions and to choose the right course of action despite our fear of the consequences. Again, the Acts of the Apostles shows us this kind of courage in the lives of the first disciples. So often it says that they "spoke with boldness" in the face of those who tried to silence them. One example: After Peter and John had healed the lame man, they were arrested and questioned by the Jewish elders, who then ordered them not to speak any more about Jesus. But the apostles replied that they have to obey God rather than human powers, "for we cannot keep from speaking about what we have seen and heard" (Acts 4:20). Later, when they were again arrested and beaten, "they rejoiced that they were considered worthy to suffer dishonor for the sake of the name [of Jesus]. And every day, in the temple and at home, they did not cease to teach and proclaim Jesus as the Messiah" (5:41-42). Undoubtedly, the disciples feared further punishment, but that did not deter them from continuing to do what they knew was their mission.

The Holy Spirit gives us the power to love as Jesus taught us. At the Last Supper he told the disciples, "This is my commandment, that you love one another as I have loved you (John 15:12). This means more than just a sweet, sentimental love. It is love in action, a sacrificial love. So Jesus adds, "No one has greater love than this—to lay down one's life for one's friends" (15:13). The first Christians took that commandment very seriously. The First Letter of John, written near the end of the first century, calls the Christians to sacrificial love: "We know love by this, that he (Christ) laid down his life for us—and we ought to lay down our lives for one another" (1 John 3:16).

Sacrificial love does not come easily to us. It goes beyond the mutuality that often exists between people who see the good in each other and have come to care about each other. It calls us to love even when there is no mutuality, when the other does not reciprocate or even rejects our love. Sometimes it requires us to put our own wants or needs on hold in order to respond to the other's need. It is a milder but genuine form of "laying down our life" for another. The Holy Spirit opens our eyes to the needs of our neighbor, strengthens our weak will, heals our tendency to remain in our own comfort zone, and enables us to let go of hurts and resentments that make us want to avoid getting involved with people. More positively, the Holy Spirit inspires us to write a note or pay a visit when we hear someone is sick, to ask if we can help when we see someone who looks stressed, and to pray rather than curse when someone cuts us off in traffic.

Catholics are not known for our willingness to talk about faith or share it with others.

Catholics are not known for our willingness to talk about faith or share it with others, but when we do we need not advocate an aggressive or "in your face" evangelism. That is disrespectful and irritating. As Saint Peter urged his fellow Christians, "Always be ready to make your defense to anyone who demands from you an accounting for the hope that is in you; yet do it with gentleness and reverence" (1 Peter 3:15-16). Peter took it for granted that unbelievers would notice something different about the spirit and behavior of Christians and would ask the reason for it. "Always be ready to explain, to tell the story of Jesus and all he has done for us; and how you now have a sense of peace and joy in your heart because you know who you are and the purpose of your life. But do all that with gentleness and reverence. Do not pressure, scold or demean anyone."

I suspect we Catholics don't evangelize this way mainly because we lack the courage and the skills. But the skills can be taught. I regularly offer a four-session training course for Catholics that I call, "How to Share Your Faith without Being Obnoxious." It is wonderful to see how the laity become enthusiastic about their faith and develop confidence in their ability to share it. The courage, however, is a gift of the Holy

Spirit—which we pray for but cannot acquire on our own. But why can we not begin to form our candidates for confirmation in this mentality? Sooner, if not later, they are going to meet peers who will challenge them on their Catholic beliefs and practices. They need to be able to hold their own, or at least know where to look for answers to the questions. At the same time, they can be encouraged to reach out and share their faith with peers who may be searching for something to believe in and a community to connect with. Above all, they need to form the habit of calling upon the spiritual gifts they received at confirmation.

Finally, we can gain some insights into this sacrament by looking at the rite itself. The material substance used is *chrism*, a mixture of olive oil and perfume. Since ancient times, oil has been used by athletes to strengthen and loosen their muscles. It was also a healing agent. So we are reminded that confirmation strengthens our commitment to Christ and to the church, and it heals our fears and weaknesses. It helps to recall that chrism has been held in great reverence by the church for centuries. It is blessed each year by the bishop on Holy Thursday and distributed to all the parishes in the diocese, where it is reserved in a special place for "sacred oils." Chrism is also used at baptism, at the ordination of priests and bishops to anoint their hands, and it is spread all over the altar and on the walls or pillars when a new church building is dedicated. It is a wonderful sign of "consecration"—something or someone is set aside for a holy purpose. In confirmation, the baptized Christian is consecrated to bring the presence of Christ into our world.

For the action of the sacrament, the bishop (or in some cases the pastor) places his hand on the head of the person and anoints the forehead with the chrism while saying, "Be sealed with the gift of the Holy Spirit." This is done individually for each confirmand. But before this, the bishop extends his hands over the entire group (since the time of the apostles this gesture has signified the act of calling down the power of the Holy Spirit) and prays this beautiful prayer:

All-powerful God, Father of our Lord Jesus Christ, by
    water and the Holy Spirit
you freed your sons and daughters from sin and gave
    them new life.
Send your Holy Spirit upon them, to be their helper
    and guide.
Give them the spirit of wisdom and understanding,
the spirit of right judgment and courage,
the spirit of knowledge and reverence.
Fill them with the spirit of wonder and awe in
    your presence.
We ask this through Christ our Lord.

Confirmation is a sacrament that strengthens our union with Christ and with the church. It imparts the power and the gifts of the Holy Spirit. It calls us to a life of love and service of our neighbor. And it sends us forth to witness our faith in the Lord Jesus by our example as well as by our words. Confirmation imprints "an indelible mark" or "character" upon the soul. Practically, this means that, like baptism, confirmation can be received only once. But more profound, it means that the effects of the sacrament last a lifetime. The gifts and guidance of the Holy Spirit are always available to us. All we need do is open ourselves in prayer: "Come, Holy

Spirit, fill the hearts of your faithful, and enkindle in them the fire of your love."

Reconciliation

This sacrament used to be called confession or the sacrament of penance. Both names are inadequate, because they describe only one part or aspect of the sacrament. Today it is more properly called reconciliation to highlight the total process whereby one who has sinned repents inwardly, confesses his or her sin(s), and receives forgiveness. Nowadays the use of this sacrament has declined drastically among Catholics. Gone are the long lines of penitents waiting to "go to confession." What has happened?

Many people no longer believe what they are doing is wrong or sinful.

Most people agree that this decline in the use of reconciliation is not because people are sinning less. Some blame it on the erosion of what is called "the sense of sin," that for whatever reason many people no longer believe what they are doing is wrong or sinful. Of course, this decline could also be a reaction to the earlier mindset of the church that put too much emphasis on sin and created an unhealthy sense of guilt. Also, Catholics are generally being taught that reconciliation ought to be celebrated thoughtfully rather than casually or out of mere habit.

But there is another dynamic at work here: Some people seriously question why they need to confess their sins to a priest. Why not directly to God in the privacy of one's heart?

The question is not frivolous. It deserves serious contemplation, and the answer ultimately illuminates the benefits of this sacrament to the person seeking forgiveness.

Let me begin with a story told by Archbishop Timothy Dolan. When he was a young priest in St. Louis, he and his pastor were taking a walk one summer evening when they met a prominent Jewish psychiatrist who lived in the neighborhood. He asked about an article he had read in the paper concerning the decline of confessions among Catholics. When the two priests agreed that it was also their experience, the psychiatrist said with a chuckle, "Well, that's good news for my business. People pay me well to do what you guys do in confession, and I can't even forgive their sins. All I can do is help them live with the results!"

To me that little story underlines an important truth: People still have a need to confess their sins to another human being. All that has changed is that they are not going to the priest. Who hears confessions nowadays? Psychotherapists, bartenders, hairdressers, prison fellowship groups, support groups such as Alcoholics Anonymous. People pour out not only their misfortunes, bad luck, and mistreatment by others, but also their failures, mistakes, wrong choices—yes, their sins. And they find they are not scolded or judged. They are accepted and encouraged. I even read about a telephone service in Los Angeles called "the Apology Sound-Off Line." It gives callers an opportunity to confess their wrongs to an answering machine. Every day an average of two hundred anonymous callers leave sixty-second messages. Adultery is a common confession. Some even confess to criminal acts. A recovering alcoholic left a message that said, "I would like to apologize to all the people I hurt in my eighteen years as an addict." The trouble is that none of the above are granted forgiveness. That, as the gospels remind us, can only come from God.

Now, I believe that among other things Jesus was a wise psychologist who knew we would need assurance of divine forgiveness for our sins. Recall what we said about "the sacramental principle." The saving, life-giving actions of Jesus are made present and visible to us through the church. Just as Jesus forgave sins during his lifetime, he provided a way to continue that healing activity down through the centuries. We read that on Easter Sunday night the disciples were gathered together in hiding behind locked doors. Jesus had been arrested, condemned and crucified. They were afraid they would be next. But besides fear they were also feeling a great burden of guilt. After all, they had let the Master down in his hour of need. They ran away. Peter had denied he even knew him. Now they've heard that some women had seen him alive, but they couldn't believe it. And even if he was, what if he found them? What would he say?

Suddenly, they see Jesus standing in their midst. He looks very much alive, even radiant. They're thrilled to see him—but they're waiting for a great scolding. Instead his very first words are "Peace be with you!" Those disciples knew they were forgiven. They didn't have to be afraid. Jesus was alive, and they were still his friends.

But then Jesus does something else: "He breathed on them and said to them, 'Receive the Holy Spirit. If you forgive the sins of any, they are forgiven; if you retain [hold back] the sins of any, they are retained'" (John 20:22-23). The early church interpreted this passage to mean that Jesus Christ handed on to the apostles and their successors the power to forgive sins in his name. But in order to know whether to forgive or retain, the minister needs to know what the sins are and whether the person is truly contrite and willing to work at changing his or her ways. This requires a human encounter—minister and penitent having a heart-to-heart, honest conversation. It is actually a beautiful example of the sacramental principle: something divine and invisible (reconciliation with God) taking place in a human, visible medium.

The beauty of reconciliation is that it offers personal, verbal assurance that we have been forgiven by God.

So the answer to why we should confess sins to a priest is that it fits so well with our human need to tell our sins to another human being for personal catharsis. The beauty of reconciliation is that it offers personal, verbal assurance that we have been forgiven by God.

Of course, the actual form of the sacrament of reconciliation evolved over the centuries. At first it was quite a lengthy process. If a Christian sinned mortally—apostasy (renouncing the faith), murder, and adultery were the main ones—the penitent was required to show that he or she was truly contrite. After confessing to the bishop or priest, the penitent would have to engage in a lengthy time of public penance: fasting, wearing sackcloth, standing outside the church and asking for prayers from the people entering, and so on. The penitent was not allowed to receive the Eucharist until he or she received absolution from the bishop, which took place only on Holy Thursday at the end of Lent. They were then welcomed joyfully back into the community, reconciled both

69

to God and to their fellow Christians.

As time went on and the church spread, it became more difficult to hold to this strict regimen, so the rite underwent changes. Gradually, it evolved into the form we recognize today: Absolution is granted immediately after the confession of sins, and the "penance" is performed afterward. This usually takes the form of saying some prayers or carrying out some work of mercy or charity. The rite has become more privatized so as not to create undue embarrassment for the penitent. One of the major changes in recent years has been the option of celebrating the sacrament face-to-face instead of the priest remaining hidden behind a screen. This makes the experience more of a human, personal encounter. But penitents are always free to exercise the option of using the screen.

We turn now to some practical suggestions for making the sacrament of reconciliation more meaningful and fruitful. I am basing these on my own experience of being both a priest and a penitent and on a small book by Fr. David Knight, *Confession Can Change Your Life* (Saint Anthony Messenger Press, 1984). We need to begin with a good preparation. Catholics know that this consists in "examining their conscience." But this can often be done superficially. One might read a list of the Ten Commandments and some typical sins under each one and say, "Yep, I did that. Nope, not that." This isn't bad, but it fails to get at the roots of our sins. As Knight says, we should dig deeper, seeking the cause underlying the external acts, which may be only symptoms. I have found this very helpful, both for myself and for my penitents. When I ask them, "What do you think is behind these actions of yours?" I often find they can come up with some very fine insights. If not, I ask them to spend some time (perhaps as

70

their penance) thinking and praying about this, asking the Holy Spirit to reveal the deeper roots of their sin. Knight puts it colorfully when he says, "We should be using the sacrament as a dentist's drill rather than a toothbrush!"

One other benefit of reconciliation involves the penance the priest is supposed to impose on us. In the past this was usually understood as reparation or "making up" for our sins. But a much better approach would be to see it as a help toward conversion—which, after all, is the purpose of the sacrament. That is, what action(s) could I perform that will help me make some constructive change in my life? In recent years, particularly with middle school and high school students, I will ask them at the end of their confession: "Well, confession implies that you intend to make some changes in your life. Which of these things you've confessed would you most like to work at changing?" I have been amazed at the ready and thoughtful answers they come up with. Then I simply suggest some prayer or action that will help them follow that direction. Or if there is some problem area, I will ask, "What do you think you can do about this?" Again, they usually respond with some realistic idea. If not, I will suggest something. As Fr. David Knight further says in his book, the doctor does not let the patient go without prescribing some medicine or some lifestyle change that will promote better health. We should expect nothing less when we are dealing with the state of our soul.

The truth is, I really like being a minister of this sacrament. I feel like I am acting as a physician of souls, helping people rebuild their relationships with God and with other people. That is why I favor individual reconciliation. It is an opportunity to meet people at the level of their deepest humanity and to minister to them with the care and compassion of Jesus.

One last thing to keep in mind: The priest is bound, under pain of excommunication, to keep secret whatever he is told in the sacrament of reconciliation. Of course we priests have offended God and our people in countless ways. Yet in all the history of the church there has not been a single documented instance where a priest broke this sacred "seal of confession." By the grace of God we have not violated that one. So people can be at peace when they entrust their innermost secrets in this sacrament.

In summary, Catholics see the sacrament of reconciliation as a precious gift of Christ to his faithful people. It is a unique opportunity for humility and self-honesty. Even more, it is a powerful means of spiritual conversion. It calls us to take an honest look at how we are living out our Christian life, our baptism. Remember Socrates' dictum: "The unexamined life is not worth living." So conversion will not happen if we seldom or never ask ourselves, "How am I growing (or getting stuck) in my spiritual life?" Above all, reconciliation is an event wherein we are met with the merciful, forgiving love of God. Jesus tried so hard to assure us that our God is always ready to forgive us whenever we turn away from our sins. He told that beautiful story of the Prodigal Son who, after making a sinful mess of his life, decided to return and ask forgiveness of his father. He was ready to accept just being a hired servant in the father's house. But the father came running to meet his wayward son, took him in his arms, and welcomed him home with a feast. So, Jesus says, there is great joy in heaven whenever a sinner repents and comes home to God (Luke 15).

❖ ❖ ❖

Holy Eucharist

Since the very beginning of Christianity, the Eucharist has been at the heart of Catholic spiritual life. It is without a doubt the clearest example of what we have been calling the "sacramental principle": Something material and visible points to something spiritual and invisible—in this case, the very body and blood of the Lord Jesus.

I once gave a homily in a rural parish that went something like this: I wish the walls of this church could talk. They would tell us the story of how this parish began and how this church was built. It was begun and built by many of your ancestors. As soon as they got settled on the land, the first thing they did was build a church and ask for a priest to be its pastor. They made great sacrifices to do so. Why? Because their faith was their number-one priority. When they came here from Europe, their relatives were sure that they were going to lose their Catholic faith in this wild, unknown land. But they didn't. They not only kept the faith—they also handed it on to the next generations. And that is why we are gathered here today.

The church building, of course, is not the center of our faith. Jesus Christ is. But people need a place in which to gather, and they gather in order to remember and to celebrate what Jesus did for us through his death and resurrection. He gained forgiveness for our sins, made us once again the beloved sons and daughters of God, and opened the way for us to eternal life. The Eucharist is the sacrament that enables us to remember all that and let it transform our consciousness.

The presence of Christ in the Eucharist draws us gently back to seek the things that really matter. Saint Paul reminded his converts at Corinth of what he had taught them about the Last Supper and how Jesus wants us to remember him by celebrating that ritual sacrifice until the end of time. In the oldest written testimony to the words and action of the Eucharist (c. 56 A.D.) Paul writes: "I received from the Lord what I also handed on to you: that the Lord Jesus, on the night when he was betrayed, took a loaf of bread; and when he had given thanks, he broke it and said, 'This is my body that is for you. Do this in remembrance of me.' In the same way he took the cup also after supper, saying, 'This cup is the new covenant in my blood. Do this, as often as you drink it, in remembrance of me.' For as often as you eat this bread and drink the cup, you proclaim the death of the Lord until he comes" (1 Corinthians 11:23-26).

We have ample historical evidence of the centrality of Holy Communion. The first Christians would gather every Sunday to celebrate together as a community. They changed the Lord's Day from the Jewish Sabbath (Saturday) to Sunday, the day on which Jesus rose from the dead and the same day he sent the Holy Spirit upon the apostles (Pentecost Sunday). The final structure of the Eucharistic celebrations (what we now call the Mass) evolved over time, but the basic elements have been there since the beginning. In the *Apologia* of Saint Justin the Martyr, Saint Justin writes to the pagan emperor Antoninus Pius around the year 150 and explains what Christians do when they gather for worship: They listen to readings from the apostles and prophets; then the presider explains and applies the readings in a homily; there are intercessions for the needs of the community and for others; a collection is taken; the bread and wine are brought forward, prayed over, and blessed by the presider; the bread and wine are given to the baptized, who receive it not as food and drink, but as the body and blood of Christ. Finally, the deacons take the sacrament to the sick and other members not able to attend the celebration. It sounds remarkably similar to what we have today. This continuity throughout history is one of the most powerful binding forces of Catholicism. Virtually anywhere a Catholic goes, no matter when, he or she will find a Mass that can be followed and understood easily—a comforting notion.

Anywhere a Catholic goes, he or she will find a Mass that can be followed and understood easily.

Regarding the Eucharist, there are probably two main issues that Catholics struggle with today. One is belief in the "real presence" of Christ in the sacrament. Not too long ago it was taken for granted that Catholics believed that Christ was really and truly present through the prayers of consecration in the Mass. But today it appears that many Catholics believe the Eucharist to be a "symbol" of Christ's presence, whereas church teaching is that the bread and wine are substantially changed into the body and blood of Christ, though the change is sacramental, not physical.

The teaching is based on the testimony of Scripture. In the sixth chapter of John's gospel there is an extended discussion between Jesus and certain Jews, in which he gradually claims that he himself is "the bread of life come down from heaven" and that he will give us his flesh to eat and his blood to drink (6:51-53). When they object to this kind of language,

Jesus insists: "My flesh is true food and my blood is true drink. Those who eat my flesh and drink my blood abide in me and I in them" (55-56). The other scriptural reference is in all the narratives of the Last Supper, where Jesus says, "This (bread) *is* my body; this (wine) *is* my blood." Not "represents" or "symbolizes" or "stands for."

The early church fathers consistently affirm the doctrine of the Real Presence. Saint Ignatius of Antioch, a disciple of Saint John the Apostle, wrote around the year 110 about certain heretics: "They abstain from the Eucharist and from prayer, because they do not confess that the Eucharist is the flesh of our Savior Jesus Christ." Saint Irenaeus, around 195: "He (Jesus) has declared the cup, a part of creation, to be his own blood...and the bread...as his own body." And Saint Cyril of Jerusalem in 350: "Do not, therefore, regard the bread and wine as simply that; for they are, according to the Master's declaration, the body and blood of Christ." Thus both Scripture and church Tradition prove to us that the body and blood of Christ are truly present in the Eucharist.

The other difficulty is usually expressed this way: "I can be a good Catholic without going to Mass every Sunday." That may be true of a few people. But ordinarily it does not work, at least over the long haul. After all, if our primary spiritual purpose in life is to be a faithful disciple of Jesus Christ, then we have to do what he asks us to do: "Do this in remembrance of me." Gather together as a community for Sunday worship, Jesus tells us. Listen to the truths of Sacred Scripture. Offer praise and thanks to God in prayer and song. Receive my body and blood in Holy Communion. And in that power, love and serve one another as I have loved you.

Sharing in the sacrament of Eucharist deepens and

strengthens our union with Christ. Let's recall what happens when we eat and drink physically. The food and liquid is changed. By a process of digestion they become absorbed into our bloodstream to build up muscle, bones and vital organs. They are transformed into our flesh and blood.

When we receive the real, risen Christ in the Eucharist, something similar happens. Only, instead of him being changed into us, we are the ones who are changed. We become more Christ-like. We take on his thoughts and his attitudes and his love for people and his dedication to the will of his Father. Behaviorally, we become more peaceful, more generous, more caring of others, and less focused on ourselves. If those things are *not* happening, we had better examine ourselves. Maybe we're coming to Communion only out of routine and not with a real spiritual hunger. The Eucharist ought to move us outward, toward helping people. As Mother Teresa put it so beautifully: "In Holy Communion we receive Christ under the appearance of bread and wine. In our works of mercy we find him under the appearance of flesh and blood. You see—it is the same Christ!"

Without a doubt, the devotion to the Eucharist lies deep in the psyche and spirit of Catholics, whether or not we are still active in the church. We are touched when we contemplate the fact that Christ chooses to abide with us in such a simple, humble form. I will never forget a scene from the Hawaiian Public Television drama *Damien*, based on the life of Blessed Damien of Molokai. The bishop and Damien were concluding a brief visit to the leper colony. As they were leaving, the lepers begged the bishop to send them a resident priest. The bishop replied that he could not ask that of his priests. Once they came to the island, they would certainly die there of the disease. But Fr. Damien spoke up, "Your Excellency, I beg you, let me come. They need the sacraments. They need to know that God, at least, has not abandoned them!" Everyone else had: their families, the government, the health department. Reluctantly, the bishop agreed to send Damien. For sixteen years, until he died there, he labored tirelessly among the lepers, helping them get clean drinking water and grow their own food, bathing their wounds and, above all, bringing them spiritual comfort. The center of the colony was the small chapel he built. There the Blessed Sacrament was kept, with the sanctuary lamp burning brightly to remind the lepers that God had not abandoned them and through the Eucharist would always be with them.

Anointing of the Sick

For many years this sacrament was badly named: "Extreme Unction." Few people knew the meaning of the word "unction" (anointing with oil) and the word "extreme" came to be interpreted as "final." As a result, the sacrament took on the meaning that "This person is at death's door—better call the priest." This interpretation also holds true of the other old title for this sacrament: Last Rites.

So when the Second Vatican Council decreed that the rites for all the sacraments should be revised in order to more clearly express their true meaning, this sacrament received a complete makeover. The Council said that this sacrament is not only for those who are at the point of death but also for those who are suffering from any serious illness; therefore, when the revised rite was announced in 1972, the name was changed to "the anointing of the sick."

Once again the sacramental principle is evident here. Jesus spent so much of his time healing sick and troubled people. I once heard that one-fifth of the Gospels are about healing. Time and again we read that the heart of Jesus was "moved with compassion" at the sight of sick and suffering people. That compassion led him to extend his healing power on their behalf. It was only fitting that he would want to continue his healing action through the church. Already in the Gospel of Mark we read that Jesus sent the apostles out on mission and that "they cast out many demons and anointed with oil many who were sick and cured them" (6:13). In the book of Acts we see the apostles healing people in the name of Jesus (3:1-10; 5:12-16; 9:32-43). The Letter of James indicates there was already a ritual in place for ministering to the sick: "Are there any among you sick? They should call for the elders of the church and have them pray over them, anointing them with oil in the name of the Lord. The prayer of faith will save the sick, and the Lord will raise them up; and anyone who has committed sins will be forgiven" (5:14-15).

I believe the anointing of the sick is one of the easiest sacraments to understand. The priest's action of anointing with oil and offering a prayer is the visible sign that Christ's invisible love and healing power are now being directed to this sick person. Oil is an appropriate symbol, for many ointments and other healing medicines are made from it. The priest first places his hands on the head of the sick person and invites others present to do the same. This gracious gesture of touch reminds us those many times in the gospels when Jesus touched sick people, thereby assuring them of their dignity and that they are not excluded from the community by their illness. Then the priest anoints the forehead and the palms of the hands while saying this simple prayer: "Through this Holy Anointing may the Lord in his love and mercy help you with the grace of the Holy Spirit. May the Lord who frees you from sin save you and raise you up."

Before we look at the effects of this sacrament, it might be helpful to reflect a bit on the human reality of sickness. Certainly one thing we human beings share in common is that we all get sick. The human body, wonderful as it is, is neither perfect nor invulnerable. Moreover, sometimes we become troubled in our emotional life. We experience fear, confusion, discouragement or depression. From a theological viewpoint, there is one thing we must be clear on: Illness is not a punishment from God. It is simply part of the human condition. Our good health is a precious gift, so God wants us to take reasonably good care of it. Doctors, nurses and researchers are called to discover and make use of preventive medicine. Psychotherapists and physical and rehabilitation therapists use their skills to strengthen our minds and bodies. As the church document on the new rite for the anointing of the sick says, "Part of the plan laid out by God's providence is that we should fight strenuously against all sickness and carefully seek the blessings of good health...."

Illness is not a punishment from God. It is simply part of the human condition.

Still, sometimes we get sick. As we seek remedies to regain our health, we can use our illness to find spiritual meaning. At the same time, it is often difficult to pray and be patient when we are sick. So we hope that other people are praying for us and that the church will be there for us. One way the church can minister to us is through the sacrament of anointing.

Who should receive this sacrament? The document on the new rite says: those whose health is "seriously impaired by sickness or old age." In other words, it is not for those who have colds or a broken wrist or ankle—unless, of course, serious complications set in. But the document wisely adds, "A prudent or reasonably sure judgment, without scruple, is sufficient for deciding on the seriousness of an illness; if necessary, a doctor may be consulted." The document clarifies a number of other points:

- The sacrament may be repeated if the sick person recovers after being anointed and then falls ill again or if during the same illness the person's condition becomes more serious.
- A sick person may be anointed before surgery whenever a serious illness is the reason for the surgery.
- Elderly people may be anointed if they have become notably weakened, even though no serious illness is present.
- Sick children may be anointed if they have sufficient use of reason to be strengthened by the sacrament.
- Ordinarily, the person should be conscious during the anointing. But if it can be reasonably presumed that they would have asked for the sacrament if they were able to do so, they may be anointed.

- Though the document does not explicitly say so, it seems the anointing of the sick may also be given to those who are seriously mentally ill.

The document urges the faithful not to delay the sacrament until "the last minute." It is a sacrament for the sick, not just for the dying. If the person is already dead, the priest may not anoint. Instead, he is to pray, asking God to forgive the person's sins and graciously receive them into the heavenly kingdom.

In revising the rites of all the sacraments, the church has insisted on two points: First, that readings from Scripture be included; and second, that the rite take place, as far as possible, in the presence of the community, not just in private. The exception would be reconciliation. But even there, the ideal would be to have some sort of communal reconciliation (as is often done in parishes), even though the confession itself takes place in private. With the anointing of the sick, there should ordinarily be a group of family members and others present with the sick person. In hospitals and nursing homes, it is often possible to include some of the staff involved in the care of the person. A practice that is becoming more common in parishes is to celebrate anointing during Mass. This can be a very moving experience for those who are chronically ill but still able to gather in church. To have their fellow parishioners and ministers there with them, to listen to the special readings and prayers focused on healing, and to receive the individual touch of anointing by their priest gives the sick person an important message: You are part of our church community, and we care about you.

By receiving the sacrament of anointing, the sick person

receives "the grace of the Holy Spirit." What is being prayed for is what Jesus granted so often during his lifetime: healing. We pray that the person may get well, regain physical health, and be able to return to normal living. As such, the sacrament is the spiritual counterpart of what medical treatment is trying to accomplish at the physical level. We are whole persons, after all: body and spirit, mind and emotions. The anointing affects us on all those levels.

Even if healing is not granted, however, the sacrament serves another crucial purpose: strength for the illness. The sick often need courage, patience and inner peace. The may fall into discouragement, fear, resentment, and even withdraw from others and from life itself. In the sacrament, the grace of the Holy Spirit, the power of Christ's love, says to us: Trust in my power and in my love. Bear this sickness and all its inconveniences with patient endurance. Unite it with the sufferings I bore for you on the cross, and offer it for your purification and for the redemption of the world.

In my forty-five years as a priest, I have often seen gravely sick people rally and actually recover after the anointing of the sick. Even more, I have seen them move toward peacefulness and gentleness and gracious acceptance of their illnesses even when they do not get better. They begin to focus on issues greater than their illnesses: What does God want me to learn through this difficult time in my life? How can I benefit from it spiritually? They begin to face the reality of death with less fear and deeper confidence in God's unfailing love. If that is not "the grace of the Holy Spirit," I don't know what is.

One more point. The Scriptures and the rite speak of "the forgiveness of sins" as one of the effects of this sacrament.

This does not mean that the anointing of the sick is a substitute for the sacrament of reconciliation. If the sick person is in a state of serious sin, confession and absolution should precede the anointing. But for lesser sins and negative tendencies, the sacrament of anointing itself, through the same grace of the Holy Spirit, has the effect of forgiving our sins and opening us to the whole-person healing that Christ desires for us.

Most Catholics I have known really treasure this sacrament. They are grateful to know that when they or their loved ones get sick, when they've had an accident, or when they have to face surgery—the church is there for them. Even more, the healing power and the love of Jesus are available to them through this simple gesture of laying on of hands, anointing with oil, and the prayers of the priest and the gathered community.

Matrimony

Religious people have always regarded marriage as more than a civil or secular event. It is something sacred. The Old Testament pictures God standing over Adam and saying, "He is a splendid work of my creation, but it is not good that he is alone. I will create a companion for him." God forms Eve out of the "side" of Adam—not from his head or from his feet—to show that she is not above or below him, but equal. The Bible adds the theological comment, "Therefore a man leaves father and mother and clings to his wife, and they become one flesh" (Genesis 2:24).

Just as the practical ways in which marriage and the ways

society has viewed and manifested it throughout time have changed and evolved from one age to the next, so has the sacramental and theological understanding of marriage evolved. In the Old Testament it was seen as a symbol of God's love for the people of Israel, a sign of the *covenant* between them (Hosea 2:14-20). In the New Testament Saint Paul views marriage between Christians as a sacrament or "mystery" of the love between Christ and his body, the church (Ephesians 5:21-33). Early Christian writers also saw the presence of Jesus at the wedding feast at Cana and his changing of water into abundant wine as a sign that he blesses married love and suffuses it with the joy of his presence. For these reasons, Catholics consider marriage to be one of the seven sacraments.

While the sacrament should be celebrated in a church in front of a priest or deacon, they do not actually administer the sacrament. Instead, the church insists that the couple confers the sacrament upon each other. The visible sign of the sacramental principle here (the love between two people) points to the invisible reality (the love of Christ for all the members of his body, the church). That is why Paul, in the passage cited above, asks both husbands and wives to be subject to one another and to sacrifice for one another, just as Christ was subject to his Father and sacrificed himself for love of us.

The theological understanding of marriage has changed dramatically as well. The older canon law of the church defined marriage as a "contract" that gave the spouses the exclusive right over each other's bodies for sexual union. That obviously limited definition was changed by the bishops at the Second Vatican Council. They produced a refreshingly new definition of marriage as "an intimate communion of life and of love" (*Decree on the Church in the Modern World*, n. 48). This is much closer to the biblical notion of covenant, which engages the total lives of the two partners and forms them into "an intimate communion." While definitely including sexual intercourse, the partnership extends to sharing of thoughts, feelings, hopes and dreams; mutual care for children; working through problems and conflicts; sharing of leisure, recreational and cultural activities; helping each other toward spiritual growth. It is a holistic vision of married life.

The question of divorce has been a tough one for Catholics, especially as divorce rates in the United States have skyrocketed.

Catholic marriage is also characterized by three special qualities: fidelity, indissolubility and fruitfulness. Together these qualities work to create a beautiful and enriching marriage relationship. Fidelity is not only a sexually exclusive partnership between a man and a woman, but also a bond of trust and respect that can exist only between two people who truly and honestly love each other. This trust removes the self-doubts and deceit that can exist without such a bond.

Indissolubility also speaks to this trust. It gives a couple great comfort to know that whatever hardships they may endure together, whatever mistakes one or the other will make in their relationship, their marriage is forever.

Finally, there is fruitfulness. This means that the marriage covenant includes an openness to creating and nurturing children. The addition of children to a marriage, whether through birth or adoption, can bring a couple together in ways they could not have imagined before having children.

Of course, not all marriages can be embodiments of this trusting love. The question of divorce has been a tough one for Catholics, especially in the twentieth century as divorce rates in the United States have skyrocketed. The Catholic Church is faced with a tense dilemma. On the one hand, it wants to turn a compassionate face to those who have gone through the pain of divorce. On the other hand, the church wants to be faithful to the teachings of Jesus. A number of biblical passages speak to the eternal nature of marriage. In the Gospel of Mark, Jesus tells the Pharisees, who are questioning him on whether or not it is ever lawful to divorce and note that even Moses allowed for divorce in some cases, that Moses made these allowances "because of your hardness of heart." That is, they were divorcing anyway and Moses had to put some order and legal limits into the process. Then Jesus brings them back to the passage from Genesis, to God's original plan, where it states that a man and a woman are to form a new marital unit and become two in one flesh. "Therefore," he adds, "what God has joined together, let no one separate." A short while later his own disciples question Jesus on this. He replies, "Whoever divorces his wife and marries another commits adultery against her; and if she divorces her husband and marries another she commits adultery" (Mark 10:2-12). It is like Jesus is saying, "I have no power to end a marriage." And neither does the church.

What must be clear is that the church has never demanded that married couples stay together "no matter what." Some marriages are not only unhappy but also downright destructive to both spouses and children. So the church has always allowed couples to separate for good reasons. The church says, however, that they are not permitted to contract a new marriage unless their former spouse should die. Divorce by itself does not separate anyone from the church or bar them from the sacraments. This is a common misconception. As long as divorced people have not remarried outside the church, they are still considered full members of the church.

And here is where annulments come in. An annulment is not a divorce. It is a declaration by church authority based on solid evidence that a valid, sacramental marriage did not exist for this couple from the beginning. There was some radical flaw in either or both partners or in their relationship that made a true "communion of life and love" impossible to achieve. An annulment does not place blame on either party. It simply says: There was some major defect in this marriage that kept it from being a true covenant and a valid sacrament. There may have been some elements of a "natural" marriage but not the faith-filled, sacramental marriage the church envisions. The simplest example is the sixteen-year-old girl who gets pregnant by her seventeen-year-old boyfriend. They are pressured (or pressure themselves) to get married. It is a disaster, and breaks up after only a couple of years. It would not be difficult to show that there was a radical defect here: emotional and spiritual immaturity plus a lack of true freedom to enter into a permanent marriage bond. Other examples abound: A spouse conceals his homosexual orientation or his pedophilia tendencies from his wife before the marriage. Or a spouse conceals the intention to continue another relationship "on the side." Or a spouse's compulsive alcohol or drug addiction becomes evident only after the marriage. In such cases, after careful investigation the church may conclude that a valid, sacramental marriage did not exist and that the couples are free to contract a new marriage. Of course, it will have to be evident that the defect(s) have been remedied before any new marriages can be contracted.

When discussing annulments, people sometimes ask: Does this mean my children are illegitimate? The church has always taught that the children of a marriage thought or presumed to be valid at the time are legitimate. So in the eyes of the church, the child or children of an annulled marriage are definitely considered legitimate.

As formidable as annulments sometimes seem to be, most people who go through the process find it to be healing. They say they can finally see what was happening and why the marriage failed, and they can now put closure on it. This may involve forgiving themselves, their spouses, and others who were involved, and this can bring a sense of peace about the past and hope for the future. I would encourage any readers who find themselves in the situation of being divorced or remarried to consider the annulment procedure as a way of reconnecting with the church.

What are the effects of the sacrament of matrimony? The primary one is the ongoing presence of Christ in the couple and in their relationship. Most couples are quite aware that what they are pledging themselves to is daunting: a day-by-day effort to love each other and their children with a generous and self-sacrificing love. Each person will be unique and have his or her own set of personality quirks and defects. Conflicts are bound to ensue. External forces such as job losses or changes, poor health, financial burdens, children's misbehavior, and interfering in-laws will stress the couple's relationship. The temptation will always be to start fighting each other instead of facing their common foes together. But if they believe that Christ and his graces are available to them for the asking and that his love for them is sure and constant, they will have the strength and the motivation to keep working together on their problems. For the past twenty years, I have been conducting an annual retreat for married couples. I always stress the importance of praying together as a couple and having confidence in the power of Jesus to help them through their difficulties. Also, at these retreats we have one or two couples give a "witness talk" on how they have actually experienced God's presence and help in their marriage. That is always much more powerful than anything I as a celibate can say!

Since marriage is such a serious commitment, it is crucial that couples contemplating this sacrament be adequately prepared for it. The church today has designed programs of preparation that include not only the spiritual dimensions of marriage but also issues such as communication skills, finances, sexuality, child care, and conflict resolution. Likewise, there are a number of programs to assist couples throughout their marriages. A generation or two ago, the Christian Family Movement started bringing couples together in small groups in order to reflect on their marriages and family lives in the light of gospel values. Nowadays new forms of marriage enrichment have evolved: Marriage Encounter, a weekend retreat where couples are taught how to communicate with each other at a deeper level; Retrouvaille, a more intensive program for couples who are experiencing problems in their marriage; and weekend retreats where couples listen to talks on various aspects of marriage and then discuss the topics with one another and with other couples. In addition, every diocese has trained marriage counselors that couples may contact if they need help with problem areas. Just as Jesus was present to the young couple at their wedding in Cana, so the church tries to be of assistance to couples at every stage of their married life.

Finally, a word about sex. The church today is not hesitant to proclaim the goodness of sex between married couples. To say that marriage is a sacrament, a revelation of God's presence in the midst of the human, is to say that sex is also holy. It is a beautiful way for a couple to disclose their love for each other, to bond together at a profound level of intimacy, and to say to each other, "I give myself to you totally, just as Christ has given himself for us totally." Writer Valerie Schultz wrote a delightful article in *America* magazine titled "God in the Tangled Sheets" (July 1, 2002). She says: "Married sex may not always be glamorous and candlelit. But intercourse is the closest one can be to another human being. It is a bond, a sharing, a trust, a deeply intimate human encounter. It is no wonder that the relationship of Christ to the church is modeled on that of a groom and bride: we are to be that connected."

A profound way of saying, "Marriage is a sacrament."

Holy Orders

Every movement or organization has to struggle with the question: When the founder dies or leaves, how will the purpose and mission of the group be carried on? The first Christians had to deal with that question from the very beginning. As they reflected on the words and deeds of Jesus, it became clear that, even though he had ascended bodily into heaven, he had not really left them. He would continue to be with them through the Holy Spirit. Moreover, he wanted them to continue his teachings and his ministry in the world until the end of time (John 14:15-17; all of John 17; Matthew 28:16-20).

They also believed that Jesus had entrusted this mission first of all to the twelve apostles. Upon them, and especially upon Peter, he said he would build "my church" (Matt. 16:18; 18:18). Like any community, the church would need leaders. But as time went on, as we see from the Acts of the Apostles, the apostles delegated others to take leadership roles. These came to be known as "overseers" (later, "bishops"), "presbyters" (later, "priests"), and deacons. In the early years, the leader of the community was the bishop. His was the primary function of teaching, presiding at the Eucharist and the other sacraments, and providing good order and government. Later as the number of communities grew, the bishop would select and "ordain" presbyters to be the church's spiritual leaders and deacons to assist. There was a ritual action to this ordination, principally the imposition of hands and prayer to invoke the Holy Spirit. Later, anointing with oil was added to the rite, which came to be known as "Holy Orders."

The Second Vatican Council clarified some areas in which this sacrament was ambiguous. It declared that Holy Orders exists in three forms. The fullness of the sacrament resides in the bishop, who has the threefold ministry of teaching, sanctifying (through praying and celebrating the sacraments with his people), and governing (providing good

Like any community, the church would need leaders.

order) for the entire diocese which he leads. All three roles are seen as a ministry of service rather than power, a service exercised in hierarchical communion with the entire body of bishops united with the pope as head. The priest shares in the ministry of Christ as preacher of God's word, as minister of the sacraments, and as pastoral guide of the local community within the diocese. The Council also restored the order of deacon, which had been reduced to a transitional step toward priesthood. The deaconate is now open to laymen who may be married and are ordained for permanent service in the church. Deacons minister in conjunction with the bishop and the body of priests. They assist at the liturgy, lead Communion services in the absence of a priest, preside at baptisms, marriages and funerals, and direct a variety of charitable services on behalf of the parish community or the diocese.

Holy Orders is a vivid example of the sacramental principle. The ordained minister is a visible sign of the invisible presence of Jesus Christ. Frail and human as they are, the ordained are called to represent Christ to their people. They are to pursue a life of holiness and be willing to sacrifice their own comfort and convenience for the sake of their people's spiritual good. They are to devote themselves to the study of Scripture, so that they can proclaim the word of God with power and conviction. Above all, they need to be in prayerful communion with Christ, so that their ministry will flow from him rather than themselves. The Letter to the Hebrews says that the ordained minister ought to be able to be gentle and compassionate with those who are weak and wayward, "since he himself is subject to weakness" (Hebrews 5:2).

The words "unworthy priest" bring up an important point. Many Catholics and others have been angered or at least disheartened by the behavior of some bishops, priests and deacons, in particular by the sexual abuse scandals that have come to light in recent years. There is absolutely no excuse for this. There is no need to add any more to what has already been said by numerous commentators. I would simply want to add my own apology to the victims, their families, and the faithful who have been hurt by these sinful and irresponsible actions. The one bright spot in the whole experience is that it has prodded the church into constructive action. Every diocese and religious order must now have policies and procedures in place to prevent sexual misconduct and to deal with it effectively when it occurs. There is a heightened awareness among the faithful that will make it less likely for them to tolerate or conceal such behavior if it happens to them. Also, it is my hope that bishops, priests and deacons will be motivated to deepen their own conversion and growth in holiness. *The Catechism* concludes its treatment of Holy Orders with a moving quote from a fourth-century priest of the Eastern Church, Saint Gregory Nazianzen: "We must begin by purifying ourselves before purifying others; we must be instructed to be able to instruct, become light to illuminate, draw close to God to bring him close to others, be sanctified to sanctify, lead by the hand and counsel prudently" (n. 1589).

At the same time, other issues, such as the ordination of female priests or allowing priests to marry, have been in debate for many years. While weighing the merits of one side or another on these issues is outside the scope of this book, we must remember that the Catholic Church has a dynamic and evolving history. Many great minds have helped shape and mold our current church, just as new great minds will help shape our church for the future.

For all its tensions and ambiguities, Holy Orders remains a treasured sacrament in the church. Everyone recognizes the need for good leaders, teachers, pastors, animators of prayer, and models of Christian virtue. The church must continue to improve its recruitment of suitable candidates for Holy Orders as well as its programs of seminary formation. After all, the best advertisements for joining the clergy are happy and active deacons, priests and bishops.

When people think about what is distinctive about Catholicism, they easily think of the sacraments. No other religion, I would venture to say, takes the material world more seriously. Catholics believe that in the simple actions and words of the seven sacraments, Jesus Christ becomes present and acts within the souls of believers to nourish and strengthen their relationship with him. They do not work like magic, of course. The believer must approach the sacraments with faith and with the desire to receive what Christ wants to give us. For those who do, the sacraments are times of personal encounter with the God who came that we might have life in abundance (John 10:10).

Reason #4

Scripture

The Search for Truth

Years ago I came across a story about the first missionaries to England. I cannot vouch for its accuracy, but it made a strong impression on me. When Pope Gregory I sent Augustine and his group of monks to Britain, they came to the castle of King Ethelbert. The king welcomed them, and the missionaries explained that they had come from Rome to tell the people of Britain about Jesus Christ. The king then said: "You see these birds flying back and forth near the ceiling of this castle? They come in for a while to be warmed by the fire; then they fly out again into the cold. Our lives are like that. We come into this world by birth, we live for a few years, and then we die. We do not know where we came from, where we are going, or why we are here. Brothers, if you have any answers to these mysteries, please share them with us!" Augustine and the monks went on to tell them the story of Jesus and the teachings of the Christian religion. King Ethelbert asked for baptism, and thus began the evangelization of England.

Whether or not the story is true, I remember it because it made an important point. An essential aspect of our humanity is that we question: Why am I here? What is the purpose of my existence? What is the meaning of life? What happens after we die? Psychiatrist Viktor Frankl, after surviving the horrors of one of the Nazi death camps, wrote his now-classic *Man's Search for Meaning*. He claimed that the quest for a sense of meaning in life is one of the strongest needs of the human person, stronger even than the sex drive or the drive for power. Our minds hunger for the truth. From this hunger comes our desire for learning and our need for teachers.

The Catholic Church has always considered teaching an essential part of its mission. The New Testament clearly portrays Jesus as a teacher. He shares his knowledge of God and God's ways. He offers a vision of how his disciples ought to live. He challenges some of the pronouncements of the official teachers of his time. Furthermore, he commissions the disciples of the church to continue the mission of teaching: "Go therefore and make disciples of all nations...teaching them to obey everything that I have commanded you" (Matthew 28:19-20). He promised to send them the Holy Spirit, who would teach them and remind them of everything Jesus had taught them (John 14:26). Almost immediately after Pentecost, we find the apostles teaching about Jesus in the Jerusalem temple. Peter and John are arrested as lawbreakers and imprisoned, but they go right back to their teaching. They are arrested again and accused by the Jewish high priest: "We gave you strict orders not to teach in this name, yet you have filled Jerusalem with your teaching" (Acts 5:28). Paul's letters are filled with references to his own ministry of teaching about Christ and to his policy of entrusting others with the teaching office. In the second letter to Timothy we read, "Hold to the standard of sound teaching that

98

you have heard from me" (1:13), and "what you have heard from me through many witnesses, entrust to faithful people who will be able to teach others as well" (2:2). Then he urges Timothy to warn against self-appointed teachers who confuse people and lead them astray (4:15).

From the very beginning then, the church was concerned about handing on the teachings of Jesus Christ without distortion. However, since those teachings were not always crystal clear, individuals and groups within the church would raise questions or begin practices which seemed at variance with the "official" teaching. In such cases the matters would be referred to "the apostles and elders," who were seen to have final authority. We do not have a complete picture, but it appears that the twelve apostles and Saint Paul spent most of their time preaching and founding churches in various parts of the known world and would place these communities under the care of a group of "elders." Eventually, the locus of teaching and governing authority was given by the elders to a single bishop, who could then choose others ("presbyters") to assist him. In some places, such as Antioch, the church was governed by a single bishop (Ignatius) by the end of the first century. In other places the council of elders governed for a much longer time. The point is that the early church felt a need for some structure of authority to insure that the teachings of Christ would be preserved without substantial error.

Dissension Throughout Church History
The more the church spread, of course, the more likely it

became that questions and challenges to the teachings would arise. One of the earliest and most serious of these took place in the first part of the fourth century. Arius, a bishop of Alexandria in Egypt, was teaching that Jesus Christ was not truly divine. He was "like" God the Father, but not "equal." This "Arianism," as it was called, was vigorously opposed by bishops like Saint Athanasius in the East and Saint Hilary in the West, yet it spread rapidly and was taught by many other bishops and theologians. Emperor Constantine feared there might be a schism within the church, so he decided to settle the matter by discussion and consensus. He called a world-wide council of church leaders in Nicaea, Turkey, in the year 325. The Council of Nicaea was the first ecumenical council of the church. It ended by condemning Arianism and declared that the nature of the Son is "consubstantial" with that of the Father's divine nature. Jesus Christ is truly divine as well as truly human. Many Arians, however, refused to submit, so the heresy continued in various parts of the church. A new emperor, Theodosius, then convened the second ecumenical council, which met at Constantinople in 381. Arianism was condemned again, and the "Nicene Creed" was expanded to include belief in the divinity of the Holy Spirit. This is the same creed that Catholics pray every Sunday at Mass.

The third council was prompted by the views of Nestorius, bishop of Constantinople. He was teaching that the Virgin Mary, being a mere human, should not be called "Mother of God," a title that had been used for several centuries. She should be called "Mother of the Christ" or "Mother of Jesus." To some this suggested that there were two separate "persons" in Jesus: God and a man. The prevailing orthodox view was that Christ is one person (divine) in two natures (human and divine). A council was convened and began in the city of Ephesus in 431. Much intrigue and infighting went on, especially between the rival theological schools of Antioch and Alexandria. In the end, the council condemned Nestorius' views and proclaimed that Mary can rightly be called "Mother of God" because she gave birth to the one divine person, Jesus Christ. However, this led some to believe and teach practically the opposite point: In Christ there is only one nature, the divine. This would imply that Jesus was not truly human. So in 451, the fourth ecumenical council convened in Chalcedon, Turkey, again with much conflict of interests and personalities. The council upheld the traditional teaching: "Our Lord Jesus Christ is one and the same Son, the same perfect in Godhead and the same perfect in manhood, truly God and truly man...made known in two natures without confusion, without change, without division, without separation...."

The church, from the very beginning, had to struggle to understand and clarify the doctrines that had been entrusted to it.

The purpose of this review is to show that the church, from the very beginning, had to struggle to understand and clarify the doctrines that had been entrusted to it through the writings of Scripture and the traditions handed down. Individuals and groups could not simply believe and practice what seemed right to them with no regard for the received teachings. That could only lead to anarchy in religion. But the church had to call upon the collective wisdom of its leaders

101

as well as the guidance of the Holy Spirit in order to refine the teachings and impart them to the faithful. The early ecumenical councils were the principal means for accomplishing this.

Unfortunately, these and later councils failed to heal all the emotional wounds that had and would be suffered by the various groups. A great schism in 1054 divided the church into the Catholic Church in the West and the Orthodox Church in the East. The Protestant Reformation arose out of serious problems with the increasing ignorance and moral laxity of the clergy. When Martin Luther came onto the scene in the early part of the sixteenth century, he initially sought to reform the Catholic Church from within, focusing on issues such as the sale of indulgences and external observances and devotions as a means to sanctity instead of a more internal spirituality and Bible study. After a theological commission on Martin Luther and his views, the situation deteriorated quickly, and the rift widened beyond repair.

The Development of Doctrine
Still today many Catholics have serious difficulties with some of the teachings of the church. This comes partially out of a desire for the freedom to think and decide for themselves what they believe without condemnation from a third party and also out of abuses of authority from church leaders. Questions of personal, sexual and social morality have caused serious divisions within the church and society at large. The church pedophilia scandals of recent years have caused many to question church authority altogether.

But the abuse of the teaching role by certain individuals does not invalidate the entire role itself. This is why a good number of people have been and are drawn to the Catholic Church. Their search for religious truth has led them to the realization that there needs to be some body of teaching that can claim continuity with the apostolic church, as well as some locus of authority that can uphold and clarify the teaching with the passing of generations. This is not to deny that doctrines and practices do not evolve and develop over time. We have seen an example of this in the early debates about the two natures in Christ. Another example is slavery. The New Testament is abundantly clear that all persons have equal dignity in the sight of God. Yet the practice of slavery went unchallenged by Christians for centuries, largely because it was woven into the fabric of Graeco-Roman society. The practice was taken for granted, the only requirement being that slaves not be treated abusively. It was only later, when colonization of the New World and the infamous African slave trade began, that some Christians saw the horrible human degradation and raised their voices in protest. Finally in 1839, Pope Gregory XVI condemned slavery, not only the abuses but also the institution itself, as being contrary to the message of gospel freedom.

Many people do not realize that the church has a long history of the "development of doctrine." A perfect example of this is the church's teachings on social justice. Beginning in the late nineteenth century, the whole of Western society was changing rapidly with the Industrial Revolution. This presented the church with a new set of moral issues: the rights of owners versus those of workers, just wages and decent working conditions in places like mines and factories, child labor, and the role of government in business and industry. It was church leaders such as Popes Leo XIII and Pius XI who issued the great "social encyclicals" that gave moral direction for Catholics on these issues. Later the popes, bishops and theologians had to reflect on questions of racial discrimination and segregation, the international economic order that often created inequities between rich and poor nations, unemployment, the morality of war and of nuclear weapons, and the reality of poverty even among prosperous nations. There had been no previous teachings on these specific matters, so the leaders and theologians had to apply the principles of the gospel and church moral teaching to these concrete realities. That is how "the development of doctrine" takes

The leaders and theologians had to apply the principles of the gospel and church moral teaching to these concrete realities.

place. *The Encyclopedia of Catholicism* (HarperCollins, 1995) summarizes the development of doctrine perfectly: "The Church cannot only continue to repeat what it has received, but must strive to understand what it has received and teach it in ever-changing cultural contexts."

There is certainly a tension here. Many Catholics do appreciate the church's teaching authority ("the magisterium") as a gift that safeguards the faith from being distorted or lost altogether. These Catholics need to remember, though, that not many of the truths of faith have been finally defined. There is room for theologians and scholars to reflect, discuss and debate many aspects of church teaching. This is healthy for everyone. Nowadays many educated Catholics are reading theological and scriptural literature, doing their own pondering, and formulating their own positions. The function of the magisterium is to encourage this kind of reflection as well as to draw a framework within which to hold the debate. That is what the ecumenical councils and papal pronouncements generally do. They draw lines and say: As long as you hold to these defined teachings, you are free to think and discuss just how they fit together and what implications lie within them.

But still debate continues within the Catholic Church and among outside observers. Conservative Catholics want the church to come down harder on those they consider dissidents, while liberal Catholics want to see some teachings changed dramatically. Some conservative Catholics accuse their liberal counterparts of being "cafeteria Catholics"—that is, they pick and choose which teachings of the church they choose to follow and which they will reject. At the same time, many conservative Catholics ignore church teachings on social justice, racial equality, capital punishment, and the like. As with many things in life, neither side is altogether correct nor completely wrong. Both sides must remember that the Bible alone, without the help of Tradition, is not a sure guide. Throughout history, certain passages of the Bible, taken out of Biblical and Traditional context, have been used to support a host of repugnant issues, including slavery and genocide.

Perhaps then it is not such a bad idea to look to the church, which has learned much from centuries of experience and reflection. This is not to say that the church has a perfect record of correct decisions, but as human beings we learn from the mistakes of the past, and the Catholic Church has a long memory.

What I believe is needed most at this time is honest and genuine dialogue—between the Vatican and church scholars, between bishops and their priests and laity. We need a mutual sense of respect for each other, and we need to begin with the assumption that we are all searching for truth. In the end, because moral dilemmas are so complex and personal, we will have to make our own decisions anyway, but we will have done so in dialogue with the church wisdom and tradition.

One thing more. Sometimes Catholics resist or reject church teaching without really understanding it. It is important that they consult reliable sources. Often that effort will clear up the matter. If they still disagree, it does not necessarily mean they must leave the church. Unless it is a matter of clear church doctrine, there is room for various opinions and viewpoints in most cases. This is one of the attractive features of being Catholic: You can be "catholic" (wide, universal) and find yourself at home.

Reason #5

Stewardship
and Mission

You Are Welcome—You Are Needed

One of the exciting things going on in the Catholic Church today is the increased presence and visibility of lay people at nearly every level of church life. The past few generations of Catholics had become used to seeing priests and nuns fulfilling most of the ministries that were needed in parishes, schools, hospitals, orphanages and nursing homes. With the steep decline in religious and priestly vocations, we have had to depend increasingly on the laity to fulfill these roles.

What many people do not realize, however, is that lay ministries were the norm rather than the exception in early church history. Already in the New Testament writings, we find abundant evidence of lay involvement in church ministry. In his first letter to the community at Corinth, Paul reminds the members that there are a variety of gifts and services among them, but one Lord (Jesus) and one Holy Spirit who inspires them for the common good of all. He goes on to name some of these gifts: spiritual wisdom, healing, working of miracles, prophecy, and discernment of spirits. All together they form the one "body of Christ" (1 Corinthians 12:1-12). Likewise, Saint Peter exhorts his community: "Like good stewards of the manifold grace of God, serve one another with whatever gift each of you has received" (1 Peter 4:10). The writers are addressing not the ordained but the ordinary faithful. It is baptism itself that confers spiritual gifts upon them and calls them to service in the community. As the church became more clerical, this belief and practice began to fade. The laity became passive recipients rather than active participants in ministry. By the time of the Second Vatican Council in 1962, there was a strong movement to reverse this trend. So the bishops insisted that the gifts of the laity be recognized and called forth so that they can collaborate in building up the body of Christ.

This call has been answered admirably by countless people. Walk into a Catholic Church on Sunday and you will see lay people proclaiming the first two Scripture readings, perhaps a cantor leading the singing, male and female altar servers, and lay ministers of Communion. If there is a school, nearly all the teachers and the principal will be laity. The same is true of the director and teachers of religious education classes. The old "convert instructions" formerly given individually by the priest have been supplanted by a class of "inquirers" taught by a team of lay people. Laity are likely to be serving as business managers or even full-time parish administrators. Parish councils and committees are composed almost entirely of laypeople. Chaplains at hospitals and nursing homes may well be trained lay ministers.

I was amazed some years ago when I happened to see a bulletin from a parish in Houston, Texas. It listed no less than forty-nine different lay ministries. One was a bereavement support group for those who lost a loved one in death. Another support group was for those who lost their jobs and are seeking new employment. Another was an AIDS Respite Team that visits AIDS patients in their homes during the evening to provide a break for the primary caregiver. Another was called "Cancare" that links up with other churches to improve the quality of life for cancer patients and their families. What a wonderful way to engage the gifts of the laity and to reach out to hurting people in the name of the parish community.

One of the hardest things for people to donate to any cause is their time.

There are also stewardship programs in place in many parishes that focus on three ways members of the congregation can give of themselves: time, talent and treasure. One of the hardest things for people to donate to any cause is their time. We are all so busy these days, but that is also what makes a donation of time such a significant gift. Parishes all over the country, and indeed the world, are hungry for live bodies they can assign to a myriad of different tasks to help the parish. Some parish members, such as musicians, graphic designers, artists, web masters, and public speakers, have key talents and skills they can donate. And of course, the gift of treasure or money contributes to the well-being of a parish and also allows a parish to give back to the surrounding community with different social welfare programs.

At the same time, the Council was clear that the laity exercise their mission primarily "in the midst of the secular world," not just in church ministries. Of course, there are the obvious missionary opportunities in many developing parts of the world to help build infrastructure, fight poverty and disease, and educate people. But there are numerous ways in which the laity can live the Catholic mission in their daily lives. They can be examples of a strong work ethic and excellence at their jobs. They can raise healthy, conscientious families. They can fight poverty and crime in their communities with outreach programs. They can volunteer at nursing homes and care facilities. All this, the church insists, is the proper mission of the laity—their very vocation.

The Role of Good Church Leaders

For real effectiveness, however, lay ministries need to be directed and coordinated. The people need formation and training, both technical and spiritual. This is the function of authority, usually embodied in the pastor, administrator or pastoral team. Somebody has to exercise oversight and require accountability, lest the ministries suffer from internal division or conflict with other ministries. Using the analogy of the church as the body of Christ, Paul reminds his community: "The eye cannot say to the hand, 'I have no need of you,' nor again, the head to the feet, 'I have no need of you'" (1 Corinthians 12:21). To function well, the various ministries must honor and support one another rather than jockey for power or position. What is sought here is a core unity amid splendid diversity.

If human beings were fully converted, perhaps there would be no need for authority in the church. People sometimes long for some idealized "free" church where everyone would be guided by the Holy Spirit and there would be no need for an authority structure. Such movements have sprung up oftentimes in the history of the church. Typically, they show great promise at first, but then they tend to self-destruct because imperfect human egos collide with one another.

We know that "the tyranny of legalism" is real indeed. Too often church authorities have acted in ways that smacked more of worldly power than of gospel service. Jesus was forever trying to move his apostles away from their expectation of wielding power in his new kingdom. "Whoever wishes to be great among you must be your servant, and whoever wishes to be first among you must be your slave. Just as the Son of Man came not to be served but to serve, and to give his life as a ransom for many" (Matt. 20:24-28). Then at the Last Supper before he died, Jesus gave them that marvelous example of the leader as servant: He knelt down and washed the feet of each of his disciples. "Do you know what I have done to you?" he asked them. "You call me Teacher and Lord—and you are right, for that is what I am. So if I, your Lord and Teacher, have washed your feet, you also ought to wash one another's feet. For I have set you an example, that you should do as I have done to you" (John 13:12-15).

Over the centuries many church leaders have really tried to follow that model of authority as service. Whenever that happened the church community flourished. But many others, including some in our day, "didn't get it." They used their positions to "lord it over" others, to stifle free expression, and to enhance their own egos. Those communities tend to slump into discouragement or to rebel in passive-aggressive ways. Few things are more distressing to the faithful than to see their leaders acting in a pompous, arrogant manner.

It seems that Jesus had a twofold purpose in mind when

he gave the church a structure of authority. One was to encourage the members to recognize their own goodness and giftedness so that they would know they are valued and have a place in the church community. An excellent good way to do this is to involve the members in decision making. Wise leaders make it a point to consult their people on important matters and listen respectfully to their views. Even if the decision does not please everyone, people more willingly accept it if they know they have been heard. Thankfully, we are seeing this model of authority emerging in a good number of places in the church. Bishops, pastors and administrators are taking time to listen to their people. Again, the theological basis for this is our belief that baptism confers the gifts of the Holy Spirit upon each person; therefore, each person has some wisdom or insight to contribute for the common good.

Wise leaders make it a point to consult their people on important matters and listen respectfully to their views.

The other purpose of authority is to foster unity in the church community. As we have seen, when some central, final authority is lacking, matters deteriorate into chaos. Or the most vocal person or group takes control and fills the vacuum. Or, sadly, the community splits into various factions. This is why, as much as Catholics may dislike their pastor, bishop or pope, they do not want to opt for a leaderless community. I once heard a dynamic Protestant pastor say, "Almost everybody wants to be led. It is not fun to wander around until you self-destruct. It is fun to be part of a team that is well led." He went on to say that good church leaders have the ability to "cast a God-honoring vision" of what the community is called to and can become, a vision that gets people excited enough to say, "I want to be part of making that vision happen!" I would add, though, that the leader should not forge the vision alone. He should engage his people in the process.

Most Catholics do appreciate the gift of unity in the church. The thought of seeing it splinter into schism is abhorrent to them. At the same time, they value the fact that the church allows for diversity—of cultures, forms of music and worship, different expressions of the sacred in art and architecture. But again, there must be some boundaries, lest diversity becomes its own god. Good people will disagree on just where limits and boundaries ought to be placed. So leaders need to be prayerful people whose first allegiance is to the Spirit of God, who has entrusted them with the grace of authority.

We have seen that today's church is undergoing a rather profound shift—from a clergy-centered church to a lay-involved church. Perhaps a better way to put it is that we are becoming a more *inclusive* church. Clergy, religious and laity are working more closely together in shared ministries. In parishes, diocesan offices, retreat centers, and places of charitable services, women are taking prominent roles alongside men. Every year hundreds of young adults who have finished their college programs are recruited by religious communities for a year or more of volunteer service on behalf of poor people, both at home and abroad. For the past ten years I have conducted orientation classes for these young people, and I am inspired by their enthusiasm and generosity.

❖ ❖ ❖

A Welcoming Church

Another development is that our parishes are trying to become more welcoming. Welcoming newcomers and strangers to your parish is also a good example of living the Catholic mission.

I recall an incident from a few years ago. I was having Sunday brunch at a restaurant with a fellow friar, and we were talking about our preaching ministry. Next to us was a young couple with two small children, and I could tell they were listening to our conversation. Finally, they came over and said, "Are you preachers?" "Yes," we said, "we're Catholic priests." They said, "Great. We just came from church ourselves—the Assembly of God down the street. Our pastor is so wonderful. He tells us we should confess our sins. He's building a school for our children. He's starting Bible study now for the adults. And by the way, we used to be Catholic." I concurred that it sounded like a fine church indeed. "But I'm curious," I said. "We've always had confession of sins in the Catholic Church; we've had schools; most of our parishes now have Bible study. Tell me, what are you finding in your church that you didn't find in the Catholic Church?" Guess what they said. "The Catholic Church is so cold! Nobody talks to you. After Mass they rush out and practically run you over in the parking lot. At our church everyone is so friendly. They introduce themselves. They connect us with the leaders. They offer to help us if we need it." I had to admit they were right. But my second thought was: We can do that. It's basic human relations. Something Jesus would expect of us. I wondered how many other Catholics have left the church for similar reasons.

114

One group of people that especially needs a welcoming message is the large number of inactive Catholics—those who still consider themselves Catholic but have stopped attending church. We know from research that somewhere between one-quarter and one-third of all baptized Catholics are in this category. That is nearly eighteen million people in the United States alone. The research also tells us that many of them have some level of desire to reconnect with the church but are reluctant to make the first move. In recent years a number of parishes around the country and even entire dioceses have developed some form of outreach to inactive Catholics—programs with names like "Welcome Home" or "Catholics Returning." Typically, inactive Catholics are invited to attend a "listening session" where they may share their concerns or problems with the Catholic Church and ask questions in the presence of the pastor and parishioners who will respond to them in an open, caring manner. Many inactive Catholics are looking for signs that they will be welcomed back into the church when they are ready. Even if no one from one of these listening sessions actually returns to the church, at least they know that the parish or diocese really does care about alienated, hurting Catholics and is willing to reach out to them.

Let me conclude with a wonderful and humorous example of inclusivity. A year or so ago, the pastor of Corpus Christi parish, an inner city church in Oklahoma City, ran an ad in the secular paper entitled "What We Mean By Everyone Welcome." The ad went on to list all the people who are welcome: "Single, twice-divorced, under 30, filthy rich, black and proud, poor as dirt, can't sing, *no habla Inglés,* married with pets, older than God, more Catholic than the pope, workaholic, bad speller, screaming babies, passive-aggressive, obsessive-compulsive, tourists, seekers, doubters, bleeding hearts...OH, AND YOU!"

I loved it. It embodies the subtitle of this chapter: "You Are Welcome—You Are Needed."

Reason #6

Sinners and Saints

We Are All in This Together

Nowadays we are witnessing a curious paradox. On the one hand, the Catholic Church is perceived by many as a corrupt institution, unwilling to protect children from priests who are sexual abusers, using power tactics to keep its members in line, cloaking its financial dealings in secrecy, and being ruled by a small group of bureaucrats in the Vatican. At the same time, Sunday after Sunday millions of people around the world profess in the Creed at Mass, "We believe…in one holy catholic church." How can an institution, riddled with so much sin and failure, still be called holy?

In past generations Catholics were not so aware of their church's imperfections. As a minority group of immigrants in this country, we became defensive about the church, putting the best face on its structures and activities and pointing to all the good it was doing for people, especially those who were poor. But as we became more educated and the flow of information from the media became more abundant, we had to face the reality of sin and corrupting influences within the church. The bishops at the Second Vatican Council realized they had to deal with this reality and not retreat into denial.

117

So they embraced the paradox of the church as being simultaneously holy and sinful. It is holy insofar as its founder, Jesus Christ, is holy and has bestowed the Holy Spirit upon the church as its animating principle. Moreover, the church is holy because it is constantly nourished by the Holy Scriptures and the sacraments and because it inspires holiness in the lives of people like the saints. At the same time, the Council said, the church is made up of human, sinful persons; therefore, it is always in need of purification, renewal, and even reform. Until the end of time, the church will never be fully what Christ intended it to be. It will always be a "pilgrim church," traveling along on the road to holiness but often veering off course and then returning to the road.

> *The church is made up of human, sinful persons; therefore, it is always in need of purification, renewal, and even reform.*

This truth was emphatically proclaimed by Pope John Paul II in his apostolic letter in preparation for the Jubilee Year 2000. The Jubilee, he said, ought to be a time of joy and especially of thanksgiving to God for the profound gifts of creation and redemption. Nevertheless, he added, the Jubilee "is above all a joy based upon the forgiveness of sins, the joy of conversion." Therefore it is appropriate that "the church should become more fully conscious of the sinfulness of her children, recalling those times in history when they departed from the spirit of Christ and his Gospel and, instead of offering to the world the witness of a life inspired by the values of faith, indulged in ways of thinking which were truly forms of counter-witness and scandal" (*Tertio Millennio Adveniente*, n.

33). The pope went on to actually apologize, in the name of the church, for its part in causing disunity among Christians and for the spirit of intolerance and even violence in trying to convert people to the Gospel (n. 35). Such apologies on the part of church leaders have been virtually unprecedented. Hopefully it is a sign that the church is becoming more honest and humble about its mistakes and flaws. Of course, admissions and apologies will be meaningless unless they are followed by genuine change.

At the same time, the fact that the church hierarchy is made up of sinful and fallible human beings is also true of the church congregation at large. Every time you attend Mass you are surrounded by a dizzying array of people who live lives of wonderful holiness, people who live lives in sinful squalor, and people, like most of us, who live somewhere in between, never quite perfect but never completely sinful either. What all of us must remember is that no human is free of sin. To think that we are is itself a sin, but it is just as sinful to put on a "holier than thou" attitude. This is something we are all guilty of at one point or another—some of us, both church leaders and laity, more so than others. So the next time you attend Mass, find yourself a seat somewhere in the middle of the church and take a moment to realize how much sin and how much holiness surrounds you. We are all guided by the Holy Spirit, but we all fail from time to time.

Despite all these failures, Catholics throughout the centuries have been drawn to the church by its successes. So I would like to present two examples of people who embody the best aspects of Catholicism.

Frederic Ozanam and the Society of Saint Vincent de Paul

My first example of holiness in the midst of a secular environment is Frederic Ozanam. Born in France in 1813, he attended the University of Paris to study law. This was the post-Revolution era in France, and a strong anti-Christian sentiment pervaded the university. Frederic was appalled at the way his professors openly attacked religion and especially the Catholic Church. With his keen intellect and knowledge of history, he began to challenge the professors in the classroom. Soon he was joined by a few other students, and the professors were unable to answer their objections.

One day someone invited Frederic to meet Sr. Rosalie, a nun who was working with the poor in the worst slums of Paris. He was shocked at what he saw, and soon he and his friends were spending their free time helping Sr. Rosalie. Later the students organized themselves into "The Conference of Charity," which later became known as the Society of Saint Vincent de Paul. Meanwhile, Frederic was being gently pressured to join the Dominican Order. But as he prayed about it, he was convinced that he was called to marriage. For several years his wife shared with him the hardships of living in Paris on the meager income he received from being a substitute lecturer. But then he was granted full-time status and tenure. Frederic's main intellectual interest was trying to connect the church's teachings with the best features of the modern age, especially the values of liberty and democracy. On a practical level, besides spreading the work of the Society of Saint Vincent de Paul, he urged church leaders to take the side of the workers and the poor in their struggle for a decent living. As he wrote, "It is the battle of those who have nothing and those who have too much; it is the violent collision of opulence and poverty which makes the earth tremble." His views angered some Catholics and left him feeling isolated. By the time he died at age forty, the society he founded had spread to sixteen countries. Frederic was declared "Blessed" by Pope John Paul II in 1997. His is a fine example of using one's gifts of intellect and scholarship in the cause of truth, while at the same time remaining immersed with compassion in the lives of suffering people.

Dorothy Day and **The Catholic Worker**

A final "case study" of holiness is Dorothy Day. Born in Brooklyn in 1897, she was baptized in the Anglican Church. She attended the University of Illinois where she became aware of the plight of the poor. She did not see the so-called Christians around her caring much about them, so she joined the Socialist Party and rejected religion. She quit college and found a job writing for a socialist paper in New York. At one of the many drinking parties she attended, a young man who had been dumped by his girlfriend died in her arms from a drug overdose. Dorothy was jolted. "What good am I doing for others?" she asked; then went on to begin nurse's training. She became pregnant by a fellow student who left her and gave her money for an abortion, which she had. Then she met an anarchist named Forster who did not believe in either marriage or religion. He moved in with her; she became pregnant and gave birth to her daughter Tamar. "I felt such joy," she wrote, "felt the need to worship, to adore.... I felt that only faith in Christ could give the answer. The Sermon on the

Mount answered all the questions as to how to love God and one's neighbor." But the responsibility of parenthood frightened Forster, and he left her. Once again Dorothy was alone.

She felt a great need to be spiritually connected to a visible community.

She wanted Tamar baptized but was reluctant to become Catholic herself because she was still writing for the communist paper. Still, she felt a great need to be spiritually connected to a visible community, to pray and worship with others, and to give her daughter a way of life and teachings that she herself had missed. She saw all the faults and failures of the Catholic Church but decided to commit herself anyway. She drew great strength and comfort from the Eucharist and from attending daily Mass whenever she could. She immersed herself in the teachings of the church on social justice.

Some time later Dorothy met another Catholic radical, Peter Maurin. He convinced her to begin "a radical Catholic newspaper that will explain Catholic social teaching and bring about a peaceful transformation of society, a society where it will be easier for people to be good." She started *The Catholic Worker* in 1933. Each copy cost just one penny. (The price has not changed, and it is still being published today.) During the Depression years, Peter and Dorothy opened "houses of hospitality" for hungry and homeless people. These Catholic Worker houses are still present in many large cities. Because Dorothy consistently espoused the way of nonviolence, she became involved in the antiwar movement and was often jailed for her protests. While in jail she used to pray, "Lord, it is good for us to be here. For we are not just serving the poor—we are truly one of them." Dorothy Day had a unique ability to combine traditional Catholic piety with radical social activism. As Robert Ellsberg wrote of her, "She called on the church to recover its identity as an offense and a mystery in the eyes of the world."

We Are All in This Together

For two millennia the church has withstood wars, schisms, scandals, abuses of power, and controversy upon controversy. In that same time, it has given physical and spiritual healing to the sick, homes to the impoverished, courage to the frightened, understanding to the intolerant, and love to the hardhearted. In a way, the church's history is much like the people, clergy and lay, in every parish in the world—an embodiment of good and evil, sin and holiness. Jesus once compared the kingdom of God to a field in which both wheat and weeds grow together. This does not mean that the church can be complacent about its defects. The worst weeds can and should be rooted up. But the church will never be perfect. And we do not belong to the church because we are good or holy. We belong and participate precisely because we are sinners and needy and weak and imperfect. As someone once said, "The church is a mansion for saints, but a hospital for sinners." We know we cannot overcome our problems or grow spiritually merely by our own efforts. We need help—from hearing the word of God in Scripture and praying together as a fellowship of sinners striving to become saints.

Conclusion

I have tried to present six "reasons" why people continue to be drawn to or remain in the Catholic Church, flawed as it is. Perhaps there is no better way to conclude this book than by quoting the words of Carlo Carretto, who spent the second half of his life as a contemplative in the Sahara Desert. His writings incurred the displeasure of some ecclesiastical authorities because he was critical of certain aspects of the church, especially its complacency and clericalism. But to the end he maintained his love and loyalty toward the church. "No," he said, "I shall never leave this church, founded on so frail a rock; because I would be founding another on an even frailer rock: myself." He captured the paradox, tension and mystery of the church in a more extended passage:

> How much I must criticize you, my Church, and yet how much I love you! You have made me suffer more than anyone, and yet I owe more to you than to anyone. I should like to see you destroyed, and yet I need your presence. You have given me much scandal, and yet you alone have made me understand holiness.
>
> Never in this world have I seen anything more compromised, more false; yet never have I touched anything more pure, more generous, or more beautiful. Countless times I have felt like leaving you, my

Church; and yet every night I have prayed that I might die in your warm, loving arms (*I Sought and I Found*, Orbis, 1984).

Also from ACTA Publications

Invitation to Catholicism: Beliefs + Teachings + Practices
Alice Camille

A clear, concise overview of Catholic beliefs and teachings. It offers a contemporary explanation of Catholicism that is grounded in the history and traditions of the church. ($9.95, paperback)

Confirmed Catholics Companion:
A Guide to Abundant Living
Sister Kathleen Glavich

This practical resource offers tips and reflections for deepening one's personal relationship to the Catholic faith. It integrates the use of modern conventions, including Internet websites, with the lives of saints and Catholic prayers and rituals. ($9.95, paperback)

The American Catholic Experience Series
(all books $9.95, paperback)

The Spiritual Apprenticeship of a Curious Catholic
Jerry Hurtubise

In this series of vignettes, Hurtubise explores his childhood after his father died and the experiences that made him the man he is today.

Watching My Friend Die: The Honest Death of Bob Schwartz
Mark Hare

Hare documents the lingering death of his friend to cancer in the context of their deeply held spiritual convictions.

Finding My Way in a Grace-Filled World
William L. Droel

Droel documents his move from New York to Chicago and his involvement with lay movements, urban parishes, and community organizations there.

Living in Ordinary Time:
The Letters of Agatha Rossetti Hessley
MaryEllen O'Brien

Through the letters of a woman who wrote about her experiences with the post-Vatican II church, O'Brien uncovers the lived experience of lay people in the United States.